$42.00

# Megan Boyd

The story of a salmon flydresser

This book is dedicated to
JIMMY YOUNGER senior
an inspiration to all

# Megan Boyd

The story of a salmon flydresser

Derek Mills & Jimmy Younger

MERLIN UNWIN BOOKS

First published in Great Britain
by Merlin Unwin Books Ltd, 2016

Text © Derek Mills and Jimmy Younger 2016

Merlin Unwin Books Ltd
Palmers House, 7 Corve Street
Ludlow, Shropshire SY8 1DB
U.K.

www.merlinunwin.co.uk

The authors assert their moral right to be identified with
this work.

ISBN 978-1-910723-24-1
Typeset in 13 point Minion by Merlin Unwin
Printed by Melita Press

# Contents

# Background to this Book

## BY JIMMY YOUNGER

My friendship with Megan Boyd was cemented by my wife Gloria and I both being salmon flydressers. I started my career in flydressing with the firm of Redpath of Kelso in 1955 as apprentice flydresser. When my family moved to Lochinver in Sutherland, I was employed as a part-time ghillie with the Culag Hotel and dressed salmon flies for them.

After a short time at Lochinver, William Robertson, tackle dealers in Glasgow, offered me a position with their firm and I stayed with them for several years before moving to Contin in 1964 where my father had gained the position of hatchery manager at the nearby salmon hatchery and was also ghillie for the middle Blackwater fishings. At this time I was working at the famous Altnaharra Hotel which was managed by Charles McLaren, author of the famous book *The Art of Sea Trout Fishing*.

While living in Contin, I was approached to help set up a flydressing company "Sutherland Fly" in Helmsdale and be the manager/tutor. Rob Wilson, a tackle dealer and rod maker in Brora, was a partner. After winning the professional class of The International 1969 Competition run by the Fly Dressers' Guild, I was offered the opportunity to set up a flydressing enterprise in Hong Kong. My wife, Gloria, and I lived there for six years before returning to Sutherland, this time to Durness. Here I started up my own company, "Anglercraft".

I first met Megan Boyd in 1967 (before we went to Hong Kong) and we had corresponded from afar by letter. It was only on our return to Scotland that we re-established contact with Megan, initially through my wife and the keen interest she shared with Megan in Scottish country dancing. However, Megan and I were both salmon flydressers, and it was not long before we saw a great deal of each other and I would from time to time help her with her orders when she was pressed for time. So with Gloria's passion for Scottish country dancing and mine for salmon flydressing, a strong bond with Megan was soon established.

Shortly before Megan died, she passed over all her flytying material, papers and documents to me, and also her kidney-shaped dressing table at which she did all her fly-tying. Unfortunately her workshop had been left neglected for several months. Megan had simply turned the key in the door and never returned. I collected what I could in the way of feathers, etc. but unfortunately dampness and moths had taken a heavy toll and a lot of good feathers, capes and the like had to be burned. I saved what I could of the letters but some were lost. Time has passed all too quickly and we have for some years had our own business "Anglercraft" at Torthorwald in Dumfriesshire and because of pressure of work I have never had time to put to paper an account of dear Megan's life and work, much as I would have liked to.

However, the opportunity has now arisen through the kind offer of Derek Mills whom I met through my father while in Contin. Derek was at that time in charge of a salmon research scheme centred on the Conon Basin. We often went fishing together and came to know each other quite well and have kept in touch over the last 50 years. I passed all the documents, photos etc. to Derek and this book is the result.

I feel that we have now paid our respects to Megan and hope the story of her life and the tying of her beautiful salmon flies will now be even better known.

*Jimmy Younger, Torthorwald, Dumfriesshire 2016*

# Megan's Legacy

## BY DEREK MILLS

I have known Jimmy Younger and his Dad (also called Jimmy) since the early 1960s and we all went fishing together fairly often. I came to admire the dedication that both he and his father put into flytying, rod making and other tackle manufacture. Recently I had occasion to have a chat with Jimmy over the phone and Megan Boyd's name cropped up regarding a recent film (*Kiss the Water*) that had been made of Megan's life.

Jimmy mentioned that Megan had given him all her documents, letters and photos collected by her over the years as well as the kidney-shaped table at which she used to tie her flies. Fortunately she must have been something of a hoarder as I was to find out. I suggested to Jimmy that he ought to write her biography, as it would be of great interest to many flydressers and anglers. His reply was that he had neither the time nor the inclination, so I suggested that if he liked I would be pleased to undertake the task if he were to send me all the material he had. His reply was that there was no one he would prefer more than me to write her biography. The result we hoped would be a book under joint authorship along with a contribution from his wife, Gloria, who knew Megan probably better than anyone.

Among the friends with whom I had fished were Richard Tyser (Jessie Tyser's son) and Neil Graesser, who bought all their flies from Megan, and so in this way I had already heard about this wonderful flydresser, and I knew it would be a pleasure assembling her life story.

A few days later the postman arrived at our house with a parcel weighing well over 10kg, and my work had started. The correspondence was gathered into bundles but in no chronological order. One thing that was immediately noticeable was that most of the letters from abroad had had their stamps removed, so either Megan was a keen philatelist or she kept them for charity: I suspect it was the latter.

It was a task knowing just how best to assemble all this information to produce an account of such an unusual life, dedicated to providing salmon anglers with the wherewithal to lure their quarry from the water.

This is now the result which we hope the reader may enjoy.

*Derek Mills*
*Melrose, Roxburghshire*
*2016*

# Chapter One

# Herself

Rosina Megan Boyd was born in Surrey, England on 29th January 1915, the youngest of three children. Her father Bill moved the family to Brora in 1918 when she was three years old. His job was as a water bailiff on the Sutherland Estate, which had the salmon fishing rights on the river from Loch Brora to the sea. He and his family: wife, two daughters and a son, lived in the small hamlet of Doll close by the river Brora.

Then, on his retirement, he moved to nearby Kintradwell Estate where he was given the use of an estate cottage. Megan's older brother became a carpenter and lived near Brora for the rest of his life. Her sister April, as a young adult, returned to England to live in Middlesex but regularly spent her summer holidays with Megan, helping with the chores and allowing Megan more time to meet her orders that were increasing all the time.

By the age of fourteen Megan had had instruction in flydressing from Bob Trussler, a Sutherland estate keeper and she soon showed a natural aptitude and an eye for colour and balance. She had already tied her first fly of almost professional standard by the age of twelve and it is said that she used the money from her first sales to go to London and buy her father a suit. So it was not long before a track was beaten to her door by anglers keen to have her beautifully-tied flies. Her life's work had begun.

By her early twenties, following the death of her father, she was living alone at Kintradwell. During the Second World War, she delivered milk in Brora and Golspie, travelling to and from her work on a motorbike. She also served as a coastguard auxiliary. During that time the north of Scotland was a protected area and she had to have a Certificate of Residence in a Protected Area that also displayed the owner's National Registration Identity Card Number.

In the archives is a letter from people called Boyd living in Canada, who wrote to Megan during the War saying they would like to send her some food parcels if she wouldn't be offended – a lovely gesture.

Once the war ended, Megan reverted to flytying on a professional basis and her time was spent tying flies for a host of customers from all over the world and particularly in the USA where her name was especially revered.

She became the absolute master of the traditional fully-dressed salmon fly, which was comprised principally of exotic feathers, and she had little time for idiosyncratic variations or 'inventions' as she called them. She only accepted the modern techniques and styles once the innovations had really proved themselves. One notable featherwing fly did in time become established on the Helmsdale River and its reputation spread to rivers far beyond, becoming known as 'The Megan'.

When, in 1967, Rob Wilson and Leo MacLean of Brora started the firm "Sutherland Fly" with Jimmy Younger as their Manager they tried to recruit Megan as Director – but she had no interest in 'production' jobs and declined.

Nevertheless, she was very helpful to them and they established a great rapport. On many occasions she helped out during the winter months tying some of the American patterns for customers such as Orvis USA. The 'Rat' series was much in demand, in various colours: Black/Silver/Rusty/Blue, etc. She said it gave her a break from the featherwing classics that, at that time, took up most of her orders.

Such was the demand for her classic flies, both for fishing and framing, that eventually Megan had a waiting list of two to three years. Her local and regular customers received preferential treatment and other orders went to the bottom of the pile. Two rows of letters/orders from all over the world were stacked at the end of her workbench. People had to write to Megan, as she never had a telephone. So orders came either by letter or by a third party who had a phone and could deliver the message to her in person.

Some orders, usually the more urgent, would come by telegram and these gave instructions as to where the flies were to be sent. Folk coming north to fish the Oykel, Shin, Cassley, Brora, Helmsdale and Naver would call at her house with their orders for the week or fortnight ahead. If she wasn't at home, they could leave their orders in a small notebook kept in a polythene bag under the bench seat at her front door stating what flies/sizes, etc. were required and to where they should be delivered or what day they would be collected.

Megan hated letting down her regular customers and would always strive to have the orders completed by the allotted time, if necessary working by the light of her gas lamp into the small hours which no doubt attributed to her failing eyesight in later years.

Her workshop was a small wooden shed next to her cottage. On one side of her bench she had a series of shelves where her feathers were kept, many in paper bags to protect them from the light and moths. On the other side her orders from customers were stored.

During the daytime she worked with natural light only, whenever possible. In the large window directly in front of her workbench was her lamp. From here she had a long view to the sea and the sands stretching along the coast.

She was held in high esteem by another famous flytyer, Dusty Miller, who visited regularly as did several of the other top flytyers in the USA such as Joe Bates and Larry Borders. Great anglers including Neil Graesser, Jim Pilkington, the McCorqudales, Pryce Jenkins and Mrs Jessie Tyser regarded Megan as the only source of their salmon flies.

Jessie Tyser of the Gordonbush Estate was particularly helpful to Megan over the years. On behalf of the Gordonbush Trustees she arranged for Megan to take over the lease on the estate cottage at Kintradwell, rent-free for the rest of her life. She did this on the death of Megan's father Bill Boyd, who had been living in the cottage (with Megan) after he retired.

The cottage at Kintradwell, overlooking the North Sea, was very isolated. Her nearest neighbours were in the tiny community of Achrimsdale about two miles away. Megan had no electricity until 1985 in either her house or workshop and she relied on bottled gas for both light and heat.

At times, local friend and fellow flydresser Jimmy Younger spent many hours trying to fix her water supply – a narrow pipe that fed water from a small burn at the top of the field behind the house that kept getting blocked by cattle knocking off the filter. Water for tea, cooking, etc. was collected in containers from one of her friends in Brora. He also spent time trying to paper rooms in a house that didn't have one remotely straight wall in the whole place, but Megan had a neat little garden with plenty of flowers.

When the Tysers sold part of the eastern portion of Gordonbush Estate to Margave Estate Ltd in 1958, Mrs Tyser notified Megan that her house had been retained in the possession of the Trustees of Gordonbush Estate and that Megan could continue to be a tenant of Gordonbush Estate as hitherto.

Megan was a well-known and popular figure in the village and around the shops, unmistakable in her tweeds and, on dressed-up days, wearing her special fly-decorated tie. Gloria Younger had been acquainted with

Megan first as they both belonged to the Royal Scottish Country Dance Society. Megan also enjoyed her "whist drives" at the Fiddle and Accordion Club where teams of four would compete. These were popular in the rural areas of Scotland and were held to raise funds for local clubs, churches and various charitable bodies. Megan helped the old people and youngsters whenever she could and was an active member of the SSPCA (Scottish Society for the Protection of Animals).

As many of her friends didn't drive, Megan would ferry them to these events. She also encouraged children and disabled people and would spend time showing them how to tie flies, giving them free flytying lessons. Her interest in the environment made her an avid supporter of various environmental bodies including the North Atlantic Salmon Fund, an international charity which purchased the netting rights, particularly at river mouths, to provide free access to ascending salmon.

Megan seldom worked on Sundays. Instead, she would take a couple of friends on outings around the neighbouring countryside to visit new places and sometimes, if some of her regular customers were staying at nearby hotels, she would deliver their orders in person.

She loved cars, although she first of all had a motorbike and then a little Austin Seven NS 847 followed later by others. Her life alone in her cottage was shared by

her little dog 'Punch'.

She had a great sense of fun and her dog Punch was often the centre of much amusement. The little dog was a favourite with children. One child called Sophie seemed to have a particular rapport with the dog and in one picture she is depicted fishing with Punch and in one of her letters to Megan she encloses a drawing of Punch, recounting her sister's fishing exploits.

There are also in the archives a series of humorous colour pictures of salmon flies playing on the name Boyd: so we have Humming Boyd, Love Boyd, Black Boyd and so on.

It would seem that all these pictures originate from a family who came to Sutherland to fish on a regular basis and who came to know Megan well. One of their cartoons depicts Megan in her plaid skirt telling a fancy lady to cover up decently!

Megan didn't drink. Some books said that she liked a dram or two but this is not true. A small sherry was occasionally taken just to be sociable, and she always had a drop of whisky in the house for certain visitors.

8

Her flytying procedure was interesting. Megan never used a bobbin-holder until she was in her eighties. Classic featherwing patterns are usually made in several stages and Megan would just work with a certain length of thread to complete one stage, then another length for the next stage and so on. Megan often tied the bodies first. If she had an order for, say, a dozen Silver Doctors she made the bodies, put them aside and then 'married' 12 pairs of wings i.e. strips of red/blue/yellow swan or goose wing feathers so they would be at hand when needed. She prepared the rest of the wing in a similar way, so each part of the wing was ready just to be added.

As any tyer of classic salmon flies will acknowledge, it takes three or four times longer to prepare the materials than it takes to tie the actual fly. Today to tie a fully-dressed, featherwing fly such as a Jock Scott, if one was to charge what is called in the profession inflated "garage prices", would cost £40–£50!

At a glance, at the prices Megan charged in the 1960s – about £1 to £2 per fly – her flies were a bargain. She never charged enough for the lovely flies she made which were photographed for books or sent to customers to be framed. It rather irked her when other tyers told her that they could charge between £10-£20 for a classic fly. She once said that she would not increase her prices in case she lost future orders from her core customers who were the fishermen who actually fished her flies.

Attempts were made to get her to increase her prices by telling her that the people who could charge these high prices didn't rely on tying flies for a living and they had the leisure to spend a week or more tying just one fly. Jimmy Younger once met an American who could take a month to make just one classic fly – everything was 'just so'. Every feather had to be correct and every turn of silver or gold rib spaced exactly with the aid of a small ruler! He even wore tight-fitting gloves to prevent oil from his fingers tarnishing the tinsels. He charged £80 for a fly! He was wealthy and didn't need the money.

Megan remarked in a letter to Jimmy and Gloria in 1977 that Joe Bates had said that top American flytyers were charging $25-50 per fly for classic flies for framing. "Muggins me was charging $4 – but I'm just not doing any more – I can't cope or spare the time for that sort of work."

Megan's flies eventually became very valuable and at a fund-raiser for the American Museum of Fly Fishing in Manchester, Vermont in 1991 one of her hairwing flies (an Irish Hairy Mary) fetched $275. Her classic fully-dressed featherwings now go for anything from $250 to $1,000.

Visitors were always welcome to Megan's cottage whether they were anglers or simply tourists or visitors to the neighbourhood. Many wrote thanking her for her hospitality and sometimes showed their gratitude in unexpected ways. For example, in the words of a Dutch couple:

*Dear Megan Boyd,*
*Please find enclosed a couple of handmade clogs. These clogs are still being used in the part of Holland where we live at the Zuider See.*
*We especially enjoyed our visit with you, as you were so kind to invite us into your house to have coffee and cake and make one of your beautiful Torrish salmon flies. We'll never forget your kind hospitality.*

A couple from Martha's Vineyard in Massachusetts in the USA sent a Christmas card in which they said that one of the highlights of their tour of the Scottish Highlands was their visit to Megan. They could not thank her enough for her 'warm hospitality' and for tying a Megan Blue that they now had framed *together with you and your darling dog.*

Another couple from Wales had this to say on opening her letter:

> *I could hardly believe my eyes, it made my day. I thank you most sincerely for your generosity to a person who was virtually unknown to you. I shall treasure your gift with reverence, and keep it in a place of honour in our little home. I am sending you a wall-plaque made of shells, which has been a hobby of mine since my retirement. Some of the shells I picked up in Bernera on the Isle of Lewis.*

There must have been constant surprises for Megan in the post. For example, a male reader of the *National Geographic* magazine from Philadelphia had read an article on Megan in one of the issues and it resulted in his writing to Megan:

> *I have a hobby of collecting lamps especially oil lamps, and I am very much interested in knowing if a lamp such as you use is available to purchase. I do not know if the one you use is an heirloom or not but I know I have never seen one just like it. Miss Boyd would you be kind enough to write me about the lamp that you use and also let me know if I might be able to purchase one in your community.*

Needless to say, Megan saw that he received one.

Another unusual request was from a Canadian angler for a deerstalker hat, which Megan managed to source and have sent to him.

It is perhaps surprising that Megan was not an angler. In fact she thought most of us fishers were slightly dotty and in the nicest possible way she once said that 'her flies caught fish and she caught anglers'. But as Rob Wilson, part-owner of "Sutherland Fly", once remarked:

*"Whatever she thought, prince and pauper had the same treatment. It could be said that although she dallied with Peter Ross, Willie Gunn, Wilkinson and a Green Highlander, she walked with Kings".*

# CHAPTER TWO

# Her River

*You can read the river far more easily than another human being; for any chance of learning, cast your line into unexpected pools, into ignored angles of flow, questions that can't be answered: why do salmon take the fly? Why did she take the fly?*
– Gareth Evans, *Kiss the Water*

Megan grew up beside the River Brora near Doll where her father was employed as a ghillie. The river must have played some part in Megan's young life. The ever-changing moods of the river throughout the year could not go unnoticed and must have had some influence on her choice of career, so a short account of the river Brora's nature and journey to the sea will not go amiss.

The Brora is considered to be one of the best salmon rivers in Sutherland. In its upper reaches it tends to be very rapid and rises and falls very quickly being influenced by the local rainfall. Anglers would refer to its having a flashy nature. In its middle and lower region it flows more slowly having had the cushioning effect of Loch Brora.

It rises in the hills of east Sutherland and wends a rocky course down Strath Brora through the deer forests of Dalnessie and Ben Armine past the shooting lodges of Dalreavoch and Scibercross, a distance some 15 miles, before being joined on the left bank by the Black Water. Balnacoil Lodge overlooks the junction of these two rivers.

From this point the river Brora, now increased in size, meanders slowly through a succession of runs and deep pools, many of which were created by Gordonbush Estate, and flows through fairly flat rough grassland into Loch Brora. Loch Brora is three and a half miles long and half a mile wide at its widest point and has three main basins connected by the Killin and Carrol narrows. It has an average depth of 22 feet and a maximum depth of 93 feet. Gordonbush Lodge overlooks the loch on the north bank with its grouse moors and deer forests lying beneath Col-bheinn. On the south shore is Uppat House with Ben Horn towering behind it.

The final three-mile descent from the loch to the estuary is through rough pasture and arable land. The river here is boulder-strewn and has long deep pools alternating with fast rapids. Just before passing through the town of Brora, the river flows through what was the only coal mine in Sutherland, which is situated above a deep cutting about half a mile long over which pass the road and rail bridges. The mine is now closed. Below these bridges the river flows out to sea over a sandy bar. It was in this lower reach that the settlements of Brochrobie, Badnellan and Doll are situated and it is there that Megan was brought up.

The main tributary of the Brora is the Blackwater. The Blackwater is in fact larger than the Brora and drains an appreciable part of the Brora's 165-square-mile catchment. It rises in the mountains of Borrobol, Ben Armine and Kildonan deer forests and really begins where the Skinsdale, Seilga and Corriefrois burns join. Below this point, the Blackwater flows through a narrow, rocky gorge with deep pots and pools for a distance of three miles

It cascades over the Balnacoil Falls and flows on to the confluence with the Brora, a quarter of a mile below at the well-known salmon-holding pool, the Pheadair.

The part of the river Blackwater below the falls at Balnacoil and the river Brora from the confluence with the Blackwater to Loch Brora belonged to the Tyser family who lived at Gordonbush. Jessie Tyser was recorded achieving phenomenal catches of salmon. Thrice on the Brora Jessie Tyser accounted for twenty-one salmon in one day and once she caught twenty-two. She never caught the largest salmon on the estate. These were taken from the Brora, weighing 44lbs and 40lbs and taken by tenants in the lower part of the Brora. Jessie's largest salmon weighed 29½lbs.

Such catches, sadly, could never be achieved nowadays. It is now the practice to return all fish caught to the river.

# Chapter Three

# The Commercial Side

*When pre-occupations become an occupation; a vocation...How many years at the end of a road, working the feathers toward art?*
*– Gareth Evans, Kiss the Water*

One tends to forget about the side of a business which relies on a supplier providing the goods or equipment to enable the enterprise to thrive. So it is with flytying which requires all the hooks, threads, tinsels, furs and feathers. Some of the feathers, in the case of traditional salmon flies, came from the plumage of exotic birds and had to be imported, often under licence.

Megan received a copy of a letter on 14th December 1946, from Parliamentary Private Secretary Barbara Castle, to E.L. Gander Dower, Esq., M.P., House of Commons, in which she says:

*I am writing in reply to your letter of the 21st November with which you sent me the enclosed letter from Miss Megan Boyd about the import of feathers for the manufacture of fishing flies.*

*You will be glad to know that in reply to her enquiries, a letter was sent to Miss Boyd on the 19th November by the Import Licensing Department asking for necessary information and when we have received her reply we shall give the matter immediate consideration.*

*You may like to have a copy of the letter sent to Miss Boyd and its enclosure, which I am therefore enclosing.*

On 20th January 1947, Megan received a letter from The Controller, the Import Licensing Department, Board of Trade saying:

*Replying to your letter of a recent date, about the importation of Plumage into this country, I have to suggest you now contact E. Veniard, 138 Northwood Road, Thornton Heath, who are importers of the above commodity, and will give you the information you require.*

In a letter, dated February 1947 from Veniard's, one of the country's foremost suppliers of fly-tying materials who Megan regularly used Mr Veniard says with reference to booking two jungle cock necks, *"Your business in Kenya Colony should cover the particular requirements by the Board of Trade."* Earlier in the month a letter was received from Mr Veniard in which he says:

> *Your letter of the 25th inst. To hand together with letter from the Board of Trade.*
>
> *We are importing some prohibited plumage on the Continent and if you will let me know your requirements we shall no doubt be able to supply.*
>
> *It is a condition of our licences to import that we obtain from our customers whom we supply a declaration undertaking to use the bulk of such material for expert work. At a given date you would also be requested to furnish a statement showing by value the export orders for fishing flies fulfilled.*

Megan bought most of her material from well-known firms which specialised in supplying these materials; namely Veniard, Meseena and Napier and Craig. These firms and a number of fishing tackle outlets were interested in doing business with Megan and selling her flies.

In 1950 the firm of Waterton (England) Ltd in Colchester wrote:

*I was very interested to see that you were a flydresser, and I am wondering whether we might not be able to do some reciprocal business with you. If you are interested would you let me know the price per dozen of say dry and wet trout flies, and also the price each for fully dressed salmon flies, such as Jock Scott, Thunder, Blue and Silver Doctors, etc.*

In January 1956 A.E. Rudge & Son at their Unity Works in Redditch:

*Thank you for your letter of the 15th instant together with sample salmon fly which is a really beautiful production and, to be quite candid, I have never seen better myself in all my long experience of fishing tackle, but unfortunately the price will not allow us to sell them although you are good enough to offer us 25% discount.*

Hardy Brothers (Alnwick) wrote from their shop in Pall Mall, London in 1959:

*We understand from Mr Lee, who was Manager at Farlows and is now on our staff, that you usually accepted orders for Salmon flies during the close season.*

*We would be extremely obliged if you would inform us if you are prepared to accept a stock order from our branch, to make up during the winter months.*

*Should this be acceptable to you would you please state approximately how many flies you could tie, also the price in the various sizes.*

In January 1959 J.S. Sharpe of Aberdeen had written to Megan:

*We wonder if you are still interested in dressing salmon flies. We would like help out with an American order, and, if you could undertake some of this work, we shall be pleased to receive your price lists.*

The Director and General Manager, a Mr J.C.S. Mills of Farlow's in Bruton Street, London, wrote a friendly letter to Megan in January, 1963 saying:

*Thank you very much for your letter of 25th January and for getting our flies done; we are putting these out on display now and I am sure they will sell very well.*

*What a time you must have had with your roof, but I am sure you must have been glad of it in this terrible weather. If we get any Jungle Cock of good quality, I will send you some up.*

*I expect we will come North again this year and will make a point of looking in to see you. Again, very many thanks for doing the flies for us.*

Hardy's were still doing business with Megan in 1965:

*We would be pleased to know if you are prepared to tie us some single hook Salmon Flies of standard patterns during the close season, if this is agreeable would you kindly let us know your prices for sizes 1 to 8, also the approximate quantity you could make for us each week.*

*The only contact I personally have had with you was many years ago. You accepted some stock orders, when I was with Messrs. Farlow's of Leicester Square, London.*

In June 1980 D&G Fly Dressers of Aberdeen approached Megan:

*I was given your name by a friend who knows you and said you were an experienced flydresser. I am requiring flydressers to supply me with flies to complete a large order and build up stock for next season. If this is of interest to you and would consider tying for me could you send me a list of patterns, prices.*

Some smaller firms and shops, some fairly local, placed bulk orders with Megan. One faithful customer, who I [DM] knew personally, was Bob Baddon of Urray Post Office in Marybank, near Muir of Ord. Bob provided for local and visiting anglers who fished the local rivers Conon, Blackwater and Meig:

*July 1972*

*Dear Miss Boyd,*
*There has been a big demand for your shrimp and stoat's tail flies and I am completely out of stock of No. 10s.*
*Can you possibly let me have about 3 doz. of each (i.e. no. 10 L.W. double irons) whenever you get time to tie them?*

*March, 1973*

*Dear Miss Boyd,*

*I'm sorry having delayed sending my order for flies for so long but I have only now managed to get round to it. Will you please send me the following at you convenience:*

*3 doz. No. 10 Shrimp L.W. Doubles*
    *(2 doz. Red Tails and 1 doz. Yellow)*
*3 doz. No.10 Black Brahan   "*
*3 doz. No.6 Black Brahan   "*
*3 doz. No.10 Blue Charm   "  (Hair wing)*
*3 doz. No.10 Garry   "*
*3 doz. No.10 Mar Lodge   "*
*3 doz. No.10 Stoats Tail   "  (Silver Body)*
*3 doz. No.10 Hairy Mary   "*

*I had a marvellous day on the Oykel with Mr Graesser on Wednesday last – 3 salmon each. My first a 14½ pounder.*

She also tied flies occasionally for Gray & Co. and for Macpherson's in Inverness.

Megan had enquiries from companies abroad for orders for her flies and Abercrombie & Fitch Co., possibly one of the largest and most important firms in the U.S.A. specialising in all types of sporting, camping and fishing gear, enquired in 1959 if she would prepared to be a source of salmon flies for sale in the U.S.A.

A Mrs Isobel MacAulay of the Tartan House Ltd., in Halifax, Nova Scotia, Canada wrote to her in April 1973:

*Dear Miss Boyd,*

*A friend of yours Mr MacGregor gave me your address and tells me you make Diefenbaker [the Canadian Prime Minister 1957-63] hand-tied fishing flies.*

*I have three stores, and am also immediate Past President of the National Programme Committee Women's Association and would like very much to have some of the flies. If you'll send me prices I'll gladly send a cheque by return.*

A further commercial interest in her work was shown by the firm Clapp & Treat, Outfitters to Sportsmen in West Hartford, Connecticut in 1976 on the recommendation of Icelandic entrepreneur and environmentalist Orri

Vigfusson. They were particularly interested in the traditional classic salmon flies.

Throughout the time of all these enquiries Megan had built up a large list of local customers, mostly anglers who were coming to fish the neighbouring salmon rivers. This guaranteed a long list of orders that took her all her time to fulfil. They not only included flies for fishing but some of her flies were also tied up as brooches. There is a record in January 1970 of an order from Liverpool of an order for 12 dozen brooches.

Megan gave some thought to advertising and in 1957 approached the postcard manufacturers J. Arthur Dixon Ltd. in Inverness. They took a photo of Megan tying flies and postcards were produced of this image for Megan's use. The collie dog portrayed with Megan was not her dog but it added an amusing touch to the picture.

Megan's skills were much in demand. While the School of Casting, Salmon and Trout Fishing was based in Lochinver in northwest Scotland, Megan helped with flytying demonstrations. When the School moved to Co. Mayo on the west coast of Ireland, a photograph of her collection of flies was displayed as the centrepiece of the flytying demonstration.

Another Irish contact was the Fishery Manager of the Erriff Fishery who in 1971 asked her initially to tie him a dozen Red Badger flies as this was a very popular pattern and he liked to keep "a few flies for visiting anglers". He went on to say that the river was mainly a summer fishery and the most popular flies were Thunder and Lightning, Hairy Mary, Shrimp and Goshawk and a fly that he had attached to his letter called a Black Fairy. He enclosed a cheque for £3 in 'good faith'.

In April 1980 a proposal came from one of her customers in Minnesota in which he says:

*I've had an idea popping around my head since I received your lovely letter and the fly. I don't have any details worked out but let me see if I can give you a general idea. It would be a business proposition.*

He then put forward a number of suggestions regarding Megan's flytying business. The proposer of this venture offered to take a number of flies every year, importing them for sale in the U.S.A. There is no record of anything coming of this proposal.

An article on Megan that appeared in the *National Geographic* magazine in July 1956 triggered an interesting letter from a lady Professor of Zoology at Mount Holyoke College in Massachusetts. The main substance of the letter concerned producing a book relating the natural insect to the anglers' artificial flies.

*For some time I've played with the idea of making a small book about bait flies and their living models for freshwater fishermen. I am about to ask a few American authorities whether they think there may be an interest in the kind of book that I've vaguely suggested to you. I would also like your tentative opinion about it if you are willing to risk one on the slight information I have given you.*

She refers to Ronald's *Flyfisher's Entomology*, a copy of which she had recently picked up in Foyle's in Charing Cross Road. She might well have been referred to Leonard West's *The Natural Trout Fly and Its Imitation* published in St. Helens in 1911 and reprinted in 1923. Nothing seems to have come of this suggestion.

Most businesses have official bodies that represent their trade or profession and Megan was one of several advisors to the United Fly Tyers Inc. whose headquarters were in Boston, Massachusetts. Other advisors included Joseph Bates, Geoffrey Bucknall, Belarmino Martinez, and T. Donald Overfield, Ernest Schwiebert, Alex

Simpson, Colin Simpson, John Veniard, Lee Wulf and Jimmy Younger.

There is no doubt that Col. Joseph Bates helped to bring Megan's expertise as a salmon flytyer to the notice of an international audience and made her business into an international one. This is borne out by many letters and orders she subsequently received from overseas customers:

> *I recently read the article by Joseph D. Bates, Jr. in the No.3, 1971 issue of* The Atlantic Salmon Journal *about your prowess as a tyer of salmon flies in the classic tradition...*

and:

> *...because of the laudatory comments about you and your work in Joseph Bates'* Atlantic Salmon Flies and Fishing, *I would like to buy from you about 30 of your salmon flies in different patterns, feather wing, hair wing, Spey and low water style, preferably in one size hook (#4) either single or double for mounting in a picture frame.*

Over the years Megan's reputation as a salmon flydresser spread beyond the immediate circle of salmon flytyers and salmon anglers. In 1987 she received from Carter Rae, Editorial Services in Edinburgh, a letter indicating that they were researching a book on traditional Scottish crafts:

> *I understand that you have worked for some years at the craft of flytying. Would it be possible for you to jot down a few facts about flytying? – Do you, for example, tie the classical salmon flies, or flies that are used by anglers today?*

# Chapter Four

# The Flies She Tied

Jimmy Younger writes:

## THE MEGAN BOYD

During the two years that my wife Gloria and I lived in Brora I spent many happy hours in her workshop, tying and talking flies. At that time we were both working on flies for Col. Joe Bates' book *Atlantic Salmon Flies and Fishing* which was published in 1969.

After much pushing from Gloria, who through country dancing had known Megan much longer than I had, it was decided that I would ask if I could name a fly after her and, following a discussion into her favourite colours, the 'Megan Boyd' was born.

I sent a single hook version up to Megan who, after examining it through her magnifying glass, said it was fine – except for the typical Younger G.P. (Golden Pheasant) topping tail which, she said, I always made too long. However, this was soon rectified and the following dressings are the originals, including the featherwing and tube patterns.

# DRESSINGS

## Megan Boyd – Fully-Dressed Hair Wing

**Tag:** Oval silver. Royal blue floss
**Tail:** G.P. crest. Blue and yellow hackle points
**Butt:** Black ostrich herl
**Body:** Rear third yellow seal's fur, remainder dark blue seal's fur
**Hackle:** Medium blue cock over blue seal's fur
**Rib:** Oval silver
**Throat:** Dyed blue guinea fowl (wound)
**Wing:** Several strands of blue and yellow hair, brown hair over
**Cheeks:** Jungle cock (tied long)
**Head:** Black

# Hair-Winged Dressing Instructions

Stage 1 - Wind on a layer of well-waxed tying silk down to the eye of the hook and back again, stopping level with the point of the hook. Tie in a length of oval silver and form the first part of the tag, four or five turns will suffice. Tie in a piece of royal blue floss silk and complete the tag, winding from the tinsel towards the eye of the hook.

Stage 2 – Select a suitable golden pheasant crest feather and tie in, making sure it curves upwards. Tie in two small hackle points, blue and yellow, over the tag and form the butt with two or three turns of black ostrich herl.

Stage 3 – Tie in a length of oval silver tinsel then dub on a small amount of golden yellow seal's fur. Prepare a suitable medium-blue cock hackle and tie in by the point.

Stage 4 – Form the remainder of the body by dubbing on blue seal's fur. Rib the seal's fur with five or six turns of the oval silver. Then follow the tinsel down with the blue cock hackle. The throat hackle of dyed blue guinea fowl is then wound on, remembering to leave room enough for the wing.

Stage 5 – Tie in strands of blue and yellow bucktail or other suitable hair. On top of this, tie in a bunch of medium brown bucktail. Trim away all excess hair over the eye of the hook then bind the wing tightly with well-waxed thread.

Stage 6 – Select suitable jungle cock 'eyed' feathers and tie in, one each side of the wing, extending to where the blue seal's fur begins and showing the 'double eye' of the feather. Trim any unwanted material. Form a neat head. Varnish black.

## Megan Boyd – Tube Fly

**Body**:    Same, except no tail
**Wing**:    Same
**Cheeks**:  Tips of blue guinea fowl feathers tied in on each side extending to about half way down body. Jungle cock.

# Megan Boyd – Reduced Version

On small size hooks the dressing can be reduced in the following way:
Omit the blue and yellow hackle points in the tail. Use floss silk instead of seal's fur for the body, and omit the blue body hackle.
For the throat, use a small bunch of the dyed blue guinea fowl feather.

# Megan Boyd – Feather Wing

**Body**:  As fully-dressed hairwing version *(page 33)*.
**Wing**: Matched pair of golden pheasant tippet feathers. Married strips of bustard, dyed blue and yellow goose shoulder feather. Brown mallard over (narrow strips). Jungle cock cheeks. Golden pheasant topping.

# SOME MORE FLY DRESSINGS

Throughout the book mention is made of a number of salmon fly dressings, some of which are given in the chapters in which they were mentioned, but others appear now and were found among Megan's notes and correspondence.

## Hamlin's Eyeball

(requested by Gray & Co., Inverness)

**Tag**:  Silver tinsel
**Tail**:  Golden pheasant
**Butt**:  Black ostrich
**Body**:  ½ black silk, ½ yellow
**Throat**: Grouse and jay
**Wing**:  2 tippet feathers, one strand red swan, 4 strands brown mallard
**Topping**: Golden pheasant

# Cambridge Blue

**Tag**: Gold
**Tail**: Golden pheasant
**Butt**: Black herl
**Body**: Light blue floss
**Rib**: Oval gold
**Hackle** (throat): Light blue
**Wings**: Black hair
**Cheeks**: Jungle cock

# Migdale

Presented by Megan to Lord Migdale at the time of the presentation of the British Empire Medal to Megan.

**Tag**: Silver and red floss
**Tail**: Golden pheasant and barred duck
**Butt**: Black herl
**Body**: Yellow floss
**Rib**: Blue floss with the red floss through the blue
**Throat**: 2 turns each of red, blue and yellow hackle
**Wing**: Mixed Amherst red, yellow and blue swan
**Topping**: Argus pheasant
**Cheeks**: Jungle cock, blue and yellow macaw horns
**Head**: Black

# Clydesdale or Fluffy Foot

Presented to Lord Migdale at the time of the above occasion and named after his daughter's horse.

**Tag**:    Gold
**Tail**:    Golden pheasant and tippet
**Butt**:    Brownish fawn herl
**Body**:    Brown floss with gold rib
**Hackle**: Eagle fawn and grey
**Wing**:    Amherst pheasant
**Head**:    as butt

# Judge

**Tag**:    Gold tinsel and orange floss
**Tail**:    Topping
**Butt**:    Peacock herl
**Body**:    Gold tinsel
**Ribs**:    Oval gold
**Hackle**: Golden olive
**Throat**: Claret and jay
**Wings**:  Yellow, green and red swan, bustard and
          peacock
**Topping**: Golden pheasant
**Horns**:  Blue macaw
**Head**:    Peacock herl

# Night Hawk (for a Norwegian customer)

**Tag:**  Silver tinsel, yellow floss
**Tail:**  Golden pheasant crest and kingfisher
**Butt:**  Red
**Body:**  Flat silver, ribbed oval
**Throat:** Black
**Wings:** Black turkey, topping
**Sides:**  Jungle cock and kingfisher
**Head:**  Red varnish

# Norske Lure (for a Norwegian customer)

Two double hooks on wire or gut
**Tail:**  Scarlet ibis
**Body:**  Oval silver wound without interruption from
tail to throat
**Wings:** Alternate strips of white swan and speckled
bustard
**Throat:** Large badger hackle wound in front of wings
**Head:**  Black varnish

# The Duchess

**Tag**:   Silver twist & yellow floss
**Tail**:   2 toppings: Indian crow & blue chatterer
**Butt**:   Peacock herl
**Body**:  Black silk
**Ribs**:   Silver tinsel, flat twist, black hackle wound down body
**Throat**: Jay
**Wings**:  6 toppings (large sizes dyed flame & orange swan)
**Sides**:  Summer duck
**Cheeks**: Indian crow & blue chatterer
**Horns**:  Red & blue macaw & light green parrot
**Head**:  Black

# Torrish

**Tag**:   Silver twist, yellow floss
**Tail**:   Topping and gold pheasant ruff
**Butt**:   Black ostrich
**Body**:  Lower half silver twist with yellow hackle where silver ends. Upper half dark yellow mohair, silver tinsel and yellow hackle at shoulder.
**Wings**:  Bronze turkey, strands of yellow and red swan and teal, jungle cock cheek and ostrich head

## Torrish Favourite

**Tag**: Silver twist, yellow floss silk
**Tail**: Gold pheasant topping, black ostrich
**Body**: Yellow floss silk half way, the remainder yellow and red mohair; silver tinsel all the way up; ginger hackle tied in half way; guinea fowl hackle at shoulder
**Wings**: Bronze turkey, strands of yellow and red swan and teal, jungle cock cheek
**Head**: Ostrich

## Black Brahan

**Tag**: Silver
**Tail**: Gold pheasant topping
**Body**: Red lurex, ribbed oval silver
**Wings:** Black hair

The ancient flies requested for the Canadian Fly Museum by Joe Bates and David Lank were patterns used in the past on Tweed and referred to by William Scrope in his book *Days and Nights of Salmon Fishing.*
The following dressings are taken from Megan's notes:

# Kinmount Willie

**Tail**: Yellow wool
**Body**: Turn of red wool followed by hare's ear fur and one turn of yellow wool
**Hackle**: Black cock
**Wings**: Mottled feather from under wing of teal

# The Lady of Mertoun

**Tail**: Yellow wool
**Body**: Red wool, water rat fur and little red hackle
**Round the body**: Black cock's hackle
**Wings**: Mottled feather from under wings of teal
**Head**: Crimson wool

# Michael Scott

**Tail**: Yellow wool
**Body**: Red cock hackle, black wool, hare's ear, yellow wool
**Ribs**: Gold twist
**Round the body**: Black cock hackle
**Wings**: Mottled feather from back of drake

# Meg with the Muckle Mouth

**Tail**:   Yellow or orange wool
**Body**:  Red cock hackle, yellow silk, turn of crimson wool
**Ribs**:   Gold twist, hackles mixed red, yellow & brown
**Wings**: Brown turkey tail

# Meg in her Braws

**Tail**:   Yellow wool
**Body**:   Green wool, crimson wool, brown wool mixed with bullock hair
**Ribs**:   Gold twist, furnace hackle
**Throat**: Jay
**Wings**: Bittern
**Head**:  Yellow wool

A number of flydressings were found in Megan's handwriting and one or two may be Irish patterns, particularly Fenian. The initials 'PT' were written against most of the following dressings and this almost certainly referred to Pryce-Tannatt, author of the classic *How to Dress Salmon Flies* (1914).

# Toppy

**Tail**: Yellow wool
**Body**: Red cock's hackle (small), black bullock hair followed by a turn of crimson wool
**Round body**: Black cock's hackle
**Wings**: Black feather from turkey tail with white tip
**Head**: Crimson wool

# Jockie

**Tag**: Silver tinsel
**Tail**: Topping & Indian crow
**Body**: 1$^{st}$ third golden yellow floss, remainder dark claret floss
**Ribs**: Oval silver
**Throat**: Coch-y-bonddu
**Wings**: Brown mallard
**Sides**: Jungle cock

# Gold Riach

**Body:** 1st quarter orange Berlin wool, remainder black Berlin wool
**Ribs:** Flat gold tinsel, oval gold tinsel & silver thread
**Hackle:** Reddish brown spey cock
**Throat:** Wigeon
**Wings:** Brown mallard (short)
**Head:** Black vanish

# Fenian

**Tag:** Silver tinsel
**Tail:** Topping and blue chatterer
**Body:** 1st quarter bright orange seal's fur, remainder
bright green seal's fur
**Ribs:** Oval gold
**Hackle:** Golden olive from green fur
**Throat:** Jay
**Wings:** Mixed tippet in strands, married strands of yellow and orange swan, florican & golden pheasant tail, married strands of teal and barred summer duck, brown mallard duck over
**Head:** Black herl

# Sherbrook

**Tag**: Silver tinsel & lemon floss
**Tail**: Topping & Indian crow
**Body**: 1$^{st}$ third pale orange floss, remainder pale blue
**Ribs**: Oval silver
**Throat**: Pale blue
**Wings**: Mixed tippet in strands, married strand of yellow, white, orange, crimson, blue dyed swan, golden pheasant tail, florican, peacock wing, married strands of barred summer duck & pintail, strips of brown mallard over, golden pheasant topping
**Horns**: Blue & yellow macaw

# The Baden Powell

**Tip**: Oval silver
**Tag**: Light blue silk
**Tail**: Topping and green parrot
**Butt**: Black ostrich
**Body**: Two parts: 1$^{st}$ – embossed silver
2$^{nd}$ – light blue silk
**Hackle**: Scarlet over blue silk
**Throat**: Light blue
**Wings**: Grey peacock, red ibis, grey mallard topping
**Horns**: Blue macaw

**Sides:**   Jay points

The inventor was Warington Baden Powell and the source was Alex Simpson from Winnie Marowski.

Another dressing, but not in Megan's hand, was found among the papers:

# The Dallas Fly

**Tag:**   None
**Body:**   3 turns of yellow Berlin wool followed by black wool
**Ribs:**   Silver tinsel, gold tinsel (oval narrow) red thread and blue all running an equal distance apart
**Hackle:** A black Spey cock's hackle from end of body but wound the reverse way and so crossing over the ribs
**Throat:** A red hackle from the Golden Pheasant
**Wings:** Two strips of plain cinnamon turkey
**Head:**   Orange wool pecked out

# The Jubilee Fly

This was the winning fly of the Fly Dressers' Guild Jubilee flytying Competition in 1977. The winner was Mr Freddie Riley of London. The dressing was based on the Queen's racing colours – black cap, gold tassel, blue body and blue and buff striped sleeves.

**Tag**: Silver tinsel
**Tail**: A topping and tip of red hackle
**Butt**: Pale blue ostrich herl
**Ribs**: Peacock blue lurex, reinforced on either side with silver and gold tinsel
**Throat hackle**: Royal blue
**Wings**: Red, white, blue, black, blue, buff, blue goose with florican bustard in that order
**Sides**: Teal with bronze mallard over
**Cheeks**: Jungle cock or substitute and a topping overall
**Head**: Black varnish

# CHAPTER FIVE

# Fellow Flytyers

Megan made many friends among fellow salmon flytyers and a particularly interesting letter in January 1952 came from a fellow professional lady flydresser, Bessie Brown, who lived in Royal Deeside. It is worth quoting the greater part of her letter as it will be of interest to many anglers, particularly those that fish the Aberdeenshire Dee. In many ways Bessie's life mirrors Megan's own experiences:

*I am pleased to hear you enjoy flytying. It certainly is a very nice job and I think I would still like to do it, even if I had my life to begin again in different circumstances. I like knitting also and my other hobby is playing the pipes as my family are also musical and my brother is one of the King's Pipers at Balmoral and won the Gold Clasp last year at Inverness and he can tie a good fly when he likes but never practises it. I began on my own and have done so for many years. I have met all sorts of interesting people in that time and I think it very nice to meet these folk again when the next season comes round.*

*My Father was head ghillie on Lower Blackhall for 46 years and we still live in the same house. I only do salmon flies and the ones most favoured on the Dee are the Ackroyd, Beauly Snow Fly, Mar Lodge, Torrish, Gordon, Jock Scott and Thunder & Lightning in the spring, also the Brora is a very fine fly here in all sizes.*

*Low water flies are much used here such as Blue Charm, Silver Blue, Logie and Jeannie. The Sweep and Sir Charles are both very good. Yes, materials are very difficult to get.*

*I deal with Veniards and like you I think the jungle cock is very dear and a skin doesn't go far. I hope this friend in Luton you have got in touch with will be able to supply you with better ones. I think hooks are horribly dear as well and the purchase tax is very hard on us isn't it? I hope you have a successful season. I get plenty work and have to refuse a lot, but most of our friends appreciate anything we make. I have made lots of friends through flytying too.*

Two other well-known Scottish flytyers were Alex Simpson and his son Colin. Alex was a great collector of salmon fly patterns. In a letter to Megan, dated December 1969 he says:

*After three years searching I managed to get another salmon fly pattern yesterday. It is the Cock of Huellan Falls. Also yesterday I had a talk with a man who fished with Mr A.E. Wood of greased line fishing fame and knew him very well and also knew Dr. Baigent of trout fly fame. This gentleman I spoke with was surgeon to the late King Georges V and VI. I've been invited to his home to talk flies and Colin has to bring along his tied collection, which in three or four years will be built into an encyclopaedia of patterns and we hope the only one of its kind in the country. He (Colin) will be tying a copy of every salmon fly we know and they will be in plastic pockets so that all details of the dressing will be seen and they will be numbered to correspond with my written collection.*

Megan at her tying bench with flytying materials in envelopes laid
out in an orderly fashion and her vice and tools to hand.

Megan giving 'Punch' a lift. She was seldom without her small dog either with her on a walk, or asleep near the tying bench.

Megan with friends at a local whist drive.

Megan tying a fly with interested onlooker. This picture became a postcard used by Megan for business and friends.

A display of Megan's flies in the American Museum of Fly Fishing in Manchester, Vermont.

A 35lb salmon taken from the Upper Pot on the lower Brora on 30 May 1957 on a No. 8 Black Doctor dressed by Megan.

Megan (right) and friend as auxiliary coastguards during the War.

Megan's "banger", a 1944 *Austin 7*, which she drove with impressive speed along the single-track roads of Sutherland.

Megan at work in her flytying shed at Kintradwell where the water came straight off the hill, and heating was scant, especially in winter.

Letters from prospective customers would find their way to Megan, despite the flimsiest of addresses.

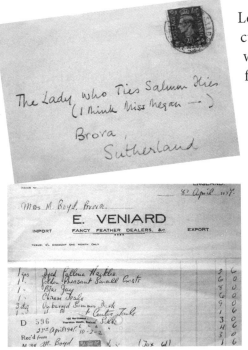

The Lady who Ties Salmon Flies (I think Miss Megan — )
Brora,
Sutherland

IMPORTATION OF PLUMAGE (Prohibition) ACT 1921

### Re Jungle Cock Necks and Peacock Tails.

We are being permitted to import from sources of supply a limited quantity of the above prohibited plumage, and as soon as they come to hand we will advise you.

The Board of Trade will require us to obtain a statement from you undertaking to use the major portion of any of this prohibited plumage you may purchase for export work. At a given date you would also be required to furnish statement showing **by value** the export orders for fishing flies fulfilled.

8 April 1957

Mrs M. Boyd, Brora.

### E. VENIARD

IMPORT      FANCY FEATHER DEALERS, &c      EXPORT

TERMS, 2½% DISCOUNT ONE MONTH ONLY

An Invoice (left) and an Importation certificate (above) from Veniards, the famous suppliers of flytying materials.

Jimmy Younger at his flytying desk

Gloria Younger, a great friend with whom Megan went country dancing.

TELEMESSAGE
MISS MEGAN BOYD

Buckingham Palace
London
SW1A 1AA

24 May 1988

I WAS VERY SAD TO LEARN THAT FAILING EYESIGHT HAS FORCED YOU TO
ABANDON THE CRAFT AT WHICH YOU SO EXCELLED. I KNOW THAT YOUR
YOUR SKILLS WILL BE MISSED AMONGST THE FLYFISHING COMMUNITY BUT
YOUR MANY FRIENDS WILL NOW BE GLAD TO SEE YOUR RETURN TO BRORA: I
DID SO WANT TO SEND YOU EVERY POSSIBLE GOOD WISH.

CHARLES.

A telegram to Megan from HRH The Prince of Wales.

With two burly friends from the States.

Young friends watching Megan at work in her shed and receiving instruction from the maestro.

The presentation of the British Empire Medal (BEM) to Megan by Lord Migdale, Lord Lieutenant of Sutherland.

A warm, welcoming smile: Megan at her tying desk as her many friends knew her.

Alex attaches a list of 84 patterns but this is far from complete and there are some obvious omissions from the Tweed.

Alex writes an interesting letter to Megan in 1976 regarding two salmon fly patterns: the Lady Gwen and Yellow Eagle:

> *The pattern for the Lady Gwen is in the book* Hair and Fur *by Thos. Glegg.*

## Lady Gwen

**Tag**: Round silver
**Tail**: Topping
**Body**: Black floss silk, rib flat silver tinsel
**Throat**: Black or bright blue
**Wing**: Lemon dyed squirrel

> *I've looked over all my dressings for a simplified Yellow Eagle and can't find one except for an American version:*

## Yellow Eagle

**Tag**: Silver
**Tail**: Golden pheasant red breast, topping on top
**Butt**: Black ostrich

**Body:**   ⅓ seal, ⅓ scarlet seal, ⅓ blue seal
**Hackle body:** Soft webby yellow hackle
**Throat:** Wigeon
**Wing:**   GP red pheasant with strip of white tipped
        black turkey either side

*As you say, Megan, this can't be done on a low water
#12 hook. Even the white tip of the turkey will be the
length of the hook so no brown will show.*

*In my next article I write for the Fly Dressers'
Guild or other magazines I'll definitely stress the
stupidity of anglers asking for a salmon flydressing
on such a small hook.*

In 1980 Bruce Zuckerman, the then-President of the
United Fly Tyers Inc. in the USA wrote to Megan
requesting her help because, he said, they were running
at a deficit and were initiating an auction to raise funds
to meet the short-fall. They had tried this locally the
previous year and raised $2000 on 53 items up for bid.
The most popular items they had were mounted flies in
shadow boxes. Three lovely stone fly nymphs donated by
Paul Jorgensen and mounted on this way fetched $400.
Bruce asked Megan if she would be willing to donate a
fly or flies that could be mounted in a similar fashion
and placed in their auction.

He said that not only would such a donation get a fine price for the club but also could, if received in good time, be used as part of the auction publicity to attract interest in the event and to help attract other gifts.

Two famous salmon flytyers in the USA were Joseph D. Bates JR and Larry Borders, both of whom knew Megan well.

Joseph Bates wrote, among many others, two significant books on salmon fishing and salmon flies. They are: *Atlantic Salmon Flies and Fishing* (1970) and *The Art of the Atlantic Salmon Fly* (1990).

He had a long correspondence with Megan and he and his wife Helen and their daughter Pam visited her at her home. Bates wrote to her often and in one letter thanked her profusely for the generous box of old flies. These were steamed by him (in order to revive the old feathers) and the single hook ones placed in separate envelopes for future framing. Among those she sent him were some double hook flies that were Forrest's patterns. These he labelled and placed in a box with cork insets so the flies could be put in without touching each other.

He frequently sent her jungle cock necks that seemed to be more readily available in the United States.

Joe framed many of Megan's flies and these were photographed and used as colour plates in his books:

*Enclosed is a photo I took of a wall on which some of the fly panels hang. These panels were framed by Will Cushner, of New York, who is a wizard at it. Each fly is mounted (with soluble cement) to a fine rod of colourless plastic set into the background, so the flies seem to be floating, and throw shadows under light.*

Joe wrote a long letter to Megan in December 1974 to bring her up to date with plans for a salmon fly museum and his discussion with David Lank, then President of the Atlantic Salmon Association, on the subject. I had met David Lank at an International Atlantic Salmon Symposium in Edinburgh. The ASA were collecting ancient salmon flies and were asking the most outstanding salmon flydressers to prepare flies for framing. They were planning 25 framed sets and hoped that Megan Boyd would agree to tie flies for four. They aimed to pay $3 per fly and the flies were to be large, usually about 3/0, so Megan was asked to do four frames at 25 flies per frame.

In a letter to Megan in January 1975 Joe stressed the importance of the salmon fly museum particularly for future generations and pointed out that she could take her time, a year or two if necessary. It is possible that Megan had some reservations about the size of the task when she had so many orders from other customers.

However, Joe was emphatic that her contributions would be most important. He told her that he had planned 26 panels of antique and modern British flies, North American flies and others around the Atlantic and people like the Simpsons (Alex and Colin), Jimmy Younger and Belarmino Martinez were contributing to the collection. He worked out how long it would take her to complete this commission and at two flies per week this would be completed in two years but he hoped that she could complete it in far less time, as he said:

> *Megan – I don't think you should refuse this. It is the chance of a lifetime to put your flies into what should turn out to be the greatest salmon fly collection in North America. It will add to your fame and will provide inspiration and education to many thousands of people. Please agree to it!*

Larry Borders was another good friend of Megan's and a tyer of classic salmon flies. He wrote her in December 1975 mentioning that he was a novice flydresser and was attempting to obtain samples of fully dressed patterns from the world's leading professionals to mount and display. He had obtained a dozen beautiful patterns from Belarmino Martinez, Spain's leading flydresser and would appreciate the following flies from her, namely the Salscraggie, Akroyd, Brora and Jock Scott.

Larry was later to become a famous flydresser himself who struck a lasting friendship with Megan.

Some time between 1975-81, Larry spent a week with Megan and would have learnt a great deal about dressing classic salmon flies: certainly he told her that he considered it the most memorable time he would spend anywhere. However, as he said in his letter of January 1981, tying flies for him was just a hobby, something he liked to do as time permitted, for relaxation. "It will never be a business with me", he said. However, he was an expert flytyer and his notepaper is headed *'Classic Salmon Flies. Meticulously Hand Made for Serious Collectors'.* He was approached by Joe Bates to tie flies for the US salmon fly museum.

At the end of the year Larry wrote saying that he was finding no time for flytying, although a letter in September 1983 suggests that he was writing articles for angling magazines and still tying occasional classic salmon flies.

Mr Joe Fandel, a former director of the United Fly Tyers, sent a short note to Megan regarding Indian crow and swan feathers and the possibility of obtaining some but was concerned about the Customs restrictions which were becoming a concern for most salmon flytyers wanting to continue dressing the classic flies.

As late as 1987, flytyers were still writing to Megan as she approached her retirement. An amateur flytyer from Northern Ireland, having seen her work at a fishing school run by Michael Walter in Pontoon, Co. Mayo in the Republic of Ireland, wrote to Megan in December 1987 saying:

*It was there that I saw some frames of your fully dressed salmon flies. I was amazed at them. They are very beautiful, the best dressed salmon flies I have ever seen.*

*I am a full time dresser myself and I am enclosing some of my own tyings which I would like you to have. Perhaps you would give me your opinion of them. I was amazed at your winging, the amount of material you had in them and also the size of your flies. Some of them were size 5/0 and possibly larger. Do you give flytying classes? I am mainly self- taught.*

He then went on to place an order. Bearing in mind that the year was 1987, it is unlikely that his order would have been met.

# Chapter Six

# Friends & Customers

*In a cottage in northern Scotland, Megan Boyd twirled bits of feather, fur, silver and gold into elaborate fishing flies – at once miniature works of art and absolutely lethal. Wherever men and women cast their flies for the mighty Atlantic salmon, her name is whispered in mythic reverence, and stories about her surface and swirl like fairy tales.*

*– Gareth Evans, Kiss the Water*

Categorising those who knew Megan as either friends or customers is perhaps unnecessary, as all her customers became her friends as will be seen from the tone of the many letters she received.

Jessie Tyser was one of Megan's greatest supporters, providing her with a house to live in and being a regular customer for her flies. However, she was no mean critic as can be seen from her letters.

There seemed to be a problem with hook condition back in 1953. In a letter to Megan from St. James's House on 7th March 1953 the sender remarks on an enclosed extract of a letter from Mr David Sealey. The extract is missing but it seemed to concern the condition of the hooks ordered. The letter goes on to refer to the numbers of hooks Sealey plans to send her and Jessie Tyser. The condition and cause of the hooks on which there was some complaint is revealed in a letter from Edgar Sealey on 3rd April 1953:

*Dear Lord Baillieu,*
*Very many thanks for your letter dated 30th March, and the hooks that you returned.*

*My Father happened to be in my office when I opened the parcel of hooks and he spotted the trouble immediately. The paper in which they were wrapped has an acidic content, and the acid corrodes very quickly any point on the hook that has not taken enough Japan lacquer. However they have washed and replated them this afternoon and they will be despatched to you this evening together with two sizes on your new order.*

There was also a problem with a slight variation in sizes particularly between the 1/0 and 2/0.

In June 1959 Jessie Tyser was interested in having her flies tied with double barbs. She sent Megan a double-barbed fly with a message that in future she would like all her single-hooked flies to be tied on a double barb light iron.

In a letter sent to Megan with an order at the end of September 1960 Jessie says:

*Would you please tie them as lightly as you possibly can? I much prefer the dressing of some of the flies you did for Mr Jim Pilkington to some of the ones you did for me in the past. I like what I call "skinny" flies.*

At the end of October of that year she enclosed in another letter a few casualties in case she could re-tie any of them.

She also mentioned that in quite a number of her nice Hairy Marys the gold wrapping of the body breaks the very first go, in rough weather or playing a fish. In that year there seemed to be quite a number of hooks bending in the most extraordinary way, either outwards or inwards.

She enclosed two Torrishes to show her: one an absolutely brand new one – one of the hooks on this bent right out, and she did squeeze it in but wouldn't trust it any longer! The same thing occurred with a small Blue Charm: in that instance, the hook had pulled practically straight out when playing a fish.

However, Jessie was also keen to help Megan in any way with her flytying and she continues in the same letter:

*That's bad news you tell me about the scarcity of Jungle Cock. I had no idea as I was fortunate enough to get six skins from India a few years ago and I have not had to buy any since the war.......*
*My son, Richard, is very keen on flytying and is really quite good so I do not want to part with all my Jungle Cock, but I have kept three skins, and if the enclosed three are what you want, by all means put their price against my flies, which I am now getting from you. I have done my best to choose skins that have a good proportion of small tapered feathers.*

Megan must have taken Jessie's comments about the quality of hooks to heart as was noticed in the correspondence from her hook suppliers apologising for the quality of hooks sent her with the promise of making sure that in future good quality hooks would be supplied her.

However, many years later I [DM] experienced similar problems with hooks provided by Neil Graesser (author of *Fly Fishing for Salmon*) when fishing the Cassley. His hooks used with tube flies were silver but were very soft and after playing a fish, the hook was no longer useable, as they were usually bent inwards, and sometimes if in a backward cast the hook should inadvertently hit the ground, the hook would be found to be bent.

Problems with hooks continued and in 1961 Jessie wrote to Megan and enclosed two to show to her what had happened to them:

*One, you see, the wretched hook (which I well know isn't your fault) has pulled straight out while playing a fish and I lost the fish! The other, you will see by the end of it was a brand new fly, and I only caught one fish on it, with this horrid result.*

It must have been very dispiriting for Megan to tie beautiful flies on hooks which occasionally let the fisher down. Two years later, in 1963 Jessie sent Megan a double-hook Hairy Mary as the barb of one of the hooks had broken and she was complaining about modern hooks generally as she frequently had barbs break off which they never used to in the old days!

*The single low-water Hairy Mary was a new one and just look at the mess it is in, after fishing with it for about an hour today!*

*P.S. Please tie all my Thunder and Lightning flies always now with a hair wing.*

Jessie Tyser was well-known as an excellent lady salmon angler and Jack Chance in his book Debrett's *Salmon Stories* says of Jessie in his chapter 'Endurance' that it was not so much the size of Mrs Tyser's fish killed at Gordonbush and Balnacoil since 1921 that attracted admiration but their sheer number. She did catch one of 29½lb but never caught one that equalled the weight of fish taken from the lower reaches of the river where tenants caught two record fish of 40lb and one of 44lb.

Not once but three times Mrs Tyser achieved the "treble" (a stag, a grouse and a salmon all in one day) – the McNab from John Buchan's famous book, *John McNab*. On 27 September, 1926, with a 7lb salmon, three grouse and a switch weighing 15 stone; ten years later on 22 August 1936, two salmon, a 13 stone stag and three grouse (also two snipe); On 30 September, 1954 a 12lb salmon, another 15 stone switch and four grouse.

Thrice on the Brora Mrs Tyser accounted for twenty-one fish in a day and one day for twenty-two. Before the war she had killed many large salmon and seatrout on the Norwegian Stryn, but it is the Brora with which her name will always be associated and esteemed.

Some of Megan's customers liked their flies dressed in certain ways, for example Mariano de Urzáiz y Silva, Duke of Luna writing from Madrid in 1956 asked for jungle cock feathers to be added to the Hairy Mary and particularly to the Yellow Garry where the contrast of the jungle cock feathers with the yellow hairs made this fly more attractive. He asked for the Hairy Mary to be tied with a silver body, as it was more attractive to salmon in Spanish rivers. He also refers to a Silver Garry.

Another customer from Spain made a number of comments on Megan's flies:

*The flies you sent look quite good (I see Miss Boyd has the same trouble as I in that it is hard to keep the teal in place over the brown mallard). I'm afraid that her 8 low water hooks are a bit small as I mentioned in my earlier letter and I would try and get some done up on # 6's requesting that particularly in the case of the Sapphire Blues, to keep the wing as thin as possible. Also in my estimation, the blue hackle used on the Sapphire Blue is too dark (although I am sure it is correctly tied according to the traditional description given in the fly dictionaries).*

*I won't bother you with any more Sapphire Blues as my good friend Rod. Haig-Brown who fished Iceland last year (1970) said that the Blue Charm was all he needed to take all the salmon he wanted.*

A customer from Aberdeen, on learning that Megan was looking for the dressing of the Poynder (sometimes known as the Captain) sent her the following dressing taken from an old book by J.J. Hardy:

**Tag**: Silver tinsel

**Tail**: Topping and Chatterer

**Body**: First half two turns light orange floss; dark orange seal's fur; dark crimson seal's fur; followed by dark blue seal's fur

**Ribs**: Silver tinsel

**Hackle**: White coch-y-bonddu dyed light red claret

**Throat**: Blue guinea fowl

**Wing**: Teal, pintail, fowl, peacock wing, Amherst pheasant, gold pheasant tail, guinea dark orange, crimson and dark blue swan; mallard, topping, jungle cock at sides

**Horns**:   Blue macaw

The customer goes on to say:

*"Any B.F. who asks you to dress this should be charged double!"*

He finishes his letter saying:

*"I hope people are losing lots of flies and are keeping you busy."*

A letter from a customer in January 1968 remarked on the prices of her flies:

*I do not know how you manage to sell them at 3/6d each, and I am sure that the Government sponsored factory will not be able to compete with either the technique or the price. Where was this government factory?*

Customers obviously felt that they got to know Megan over the years. One who had been buying her flies for some time wrote:

*Dear Miss Boyd after all these years perhaps I may take the liberty of calling you Megan.*

Sometimes friends sent her fly patterns either at her request or thinking that they might be unknown to her. Mr W.J.M. (Jock) Menzies, one-time Chief Inspector of

Salmon Fisheries for Scotland and Fisheries Advisor to the North of Scotland Hydro-electric Board and author of a number of books on salmon and salmon fishing, sent her details of one such dressing:

*Mr Edwards has asked me to send you the dressing of the Lady Amherst. The following is from a fly given me in Canada where it is a favourite on the Grand Cascapedia. It is only used in the largest sizes 3/0 and bigger.*

*It is a very old fashioned fly. I wonder where it is wanted in this country.*

# Lady Amherst

**Tag**: Silver twist and yellow floss
**Tail**: Topping and teal
**Butt**: Black herl
**Body**: Flat silver tinsel
**Ribs**: Oval silver tinsel
**Hackle**: Light badger
**Throat**: Teal
**Wings**: Two long jungle cock, two strips Amherst pheasant over lapping on each side
**Cheeks**: Jungle cock and blue chatterer
**Horns**: Macaw

# Goat's Toe

Another pattern that a satisfied customer asked Megan to dress was the Goat's Toe. He remarked that it was an interesting fly which he first came across in the south west of Ireland some years ago and which he introduced to the Hebrides where it was used as a top dropper and proved lethal to large sea trout. The dressing was:

**Tail**: Red wool
**Body**: Peacock herl
**Hackle**: Black, greenish hackle of peacock or cormorant

It was not only adults who wrote to Megan for flies and advice and a letter from a twelve-year old girl from Bridgeport, USA says it all:

*I am writing to you because I saw your picture on the page of the National Geographic Magazine. I am twelve years old and I collect fishing flies for a hobby. In your hand was a fishing fly by the name of "The Orange Parson". I was wondering about how much it costs, as I would very much like to have an Orange Parson in my collection.*

Megan received requests for her flies from a wide range of folk including Dukes (the Duke of Marlborough), Duchesses (the Duchess of Portland) and Lords (Lord Balfour of Inchrye, Lord Leverhulme and Lord Keith), Countesses (the Countess of Liverpool) and Members of Parliament. Most of them were very busy people who had little time for visiting tackle shops and so found it convenient to place their order for flies with Megan. However, Lord Balfour did send her a copy of his book on fishing *Folk, Fish and Fun,* and the Duchess of Portland wrote to Megan saying that her fly was most successful on the Tweed and she and the Duke had very good sport, catching 17 fish between them in four days.

The dressing for the Duchess of Portland fly is:

# Duchess of Portland

**Tag**:  Silver twist and turn of yellow floss silk
**Tail**:  Golden pheasant rump feather
**Body**: Darkish green mohair, silver twist or tinsel
**Shoulder**: Claret hackle with jay over
**Wing**: Brown turkey, small jungle cock cheek and two strands of blue macaw

The famous were not confined to this country and the Rt. Hon. John G. Diefenbaker, the one-time Prime Minister of Canada, wrote from Ottawa in April, 1970 that he was greatly honoured that Megan wished to call one of her salmon flies the "Diefenbaker" and the next occasion he was in Scotland he would look forward to using one of them and to meeting her. His wife was delighted with the brooch she had been given and sent her appreciation.

Two months later he wrote again to Megan saying he was delighted with the "Three little Diefenbakers" and hoped to use them during the summer recess from Parliament. His plans included a week's fishing trip in northern Manitoba as well as shorter excursions in the vicinity of Ottawa and he was placing the flies in his kit in preparation for "those restful sunny days."

Her customers could be divided into those who wanted flies to fish with and those who wanted them to frame. Probably most requests for classic salmon flies to frame came from North America, particularly from the USA. Some wanted the Big Five: Jock Scott; Green Highlander; Durham Ranger; Silver Doctor and Mar Lodge, that they could photograph and include in a book they were writing; others wanted many more to frame and exhibit in museums or their homes. The Canadian Margaree Anglers' Association in Cape Breton, Nova Scotia, planned to display in their museum Megan's flies and also photos.

The Auction Chairman of the Veazie Angling Club in Bangor, Maine, which considered itself at the time to be the only angling club in the U.S.A. to hold an annual Atlantic Salmon Banquet, wrote to Megan asking if she would donate one classic Atlantic Salmon fly for their auction. Megan fulfilled their request and in their acknowledgement they remarked that her name was mentioned often on their salmon rivers.

Sometimes orders were quite large and the following request came from an American lady who Megan had met at Strathgarve Lodge in Ross-shire:

*"In June 1970 I will be attending my 50th reunion at my university and we generally, on such an occasion, have a small gift for the ladies. If the committee would think it appropriate, would you be willing and able to make a hundred or more of those lovely pin brooches, one of which you tied for Dr. Sienewicz, for that purpose?*
*The colours should be orange and black.*

There is no record of Megan undertaking this order! However, some of her private customers took a note of the number of flies they had ordered from Megan over the years and one such lady mentioned in one of her letters to Megan:

*I have just counted the number of flies you have tied for us over the years and they number over 200!*

Others asked if Megan gave flytying lessons and in one instance enclosed examples of their work in the form of a neatly tied salmon fly. Most, however, were admirers of the flies they received and an angler from Rhode Island who was going to fish in Iceland remarked that the flies must have brought the family good luck as the day after their receipt, his wife was delivered of their first child: *'a lovely 9 pound boy – the size of a good salmon'.*

A lady coming to live at Skibo Castle in Dornoch, Sutherland, wrote to Megan asking if, as an amateur flydresser, she might come over and watch Megan tie flies and receive some instruction. This request resulted in a pleasant friendship and a thankyou letter in which she thanks Megan:

> *"for the beautiful Jock Scott that I had such pleasure in watching you tie – I did enjoy my morning with you and now hope to put into practise what I learned – there will be no excuse with the lovely feathers you also sent."*

A good Icelandic friend was Orri Vigfusson. Orri is chairman of the North Atlantic Salmon Fund (NASF). I [DM] know him quite well and had the privilege of fishing on his stretch of the Laxá ì Adaldalur in northern Iceland. He was the instigator of the buy-out of the Greenland and Faroese high seas salmon fisheries and a catalyst for the buy-out of the Irish salmon drift net fisheries.

Orri's orders for salmon flies, as far as we can tell, surprisingly did not include many Icelandic patterns such as the Laxá Blue, Blue Sapphire, Green Butt, Krafla or Francis, although Orri once sent Megan (in one of his

Christmas cards) a Laxá Blue which is a very popular Iceland fly. I doubt, in any case, whether Megan would have agreed to tie the Francis which was a monstrosity with a tapered red, green or yellow body with 2 black beady eyes and four or five wisps of red cock hackle to resemble the feelers of a deep sea prawn!

The flies in Orri's orders were two versions of the Hairy Mary, one with red brown hair wings and one with grey/white hair; other patterns included Lady Amherst, Jock Scott, the Brora, Helmsdale, the Black, Blue and Silver Doctor, Black Dose and White Wing.

Orri first met Megan in 1985 and he recalled her driving him into the village for some special biscuits to give his children:

*Though she had already turned 70 she just threw on the safety belt and drove like mad.*

Megan had a number of other Iceland customers, some having their flies delivered via the Iceland Steamship Co. Ltd. on their ship M.S. Gullfoss which used to sail from Leith in Scotland.

Joseph Hubert, a regular visitor to Iceland and author of the limited signed edition *Salmon, Salmon, with a Chapter on Iceland*, wrote to Megan from Duluth, USA in 1979 remarking that:

*The world of salmon fishing is growing smaller everyday and the ultimate conclusion is very evident. Artists such as yourself represent the last lingering glimpse of a most unique way of life for those unfortunate souls who will never fully understand what has been lost.*

He sent her a signed print of a salmon which appears in his beautifully illustrated book.

A range of accounts and incidents were related in letters to Megan from satisfied customers. One said that:

*...it might amuse you to know that in one of the worst salmon years of the last 30, those "coarse" flies you tied for me were extremely successful and I had my best back end fishing ever. I got 25 fish in 13 days mostly on the shorter tangerine and black including a cock of 28½ lbs that everybody guessed as 35-40 and certainly was 35 when he came up.*

Another customer, who had been fishing in Iceland, sent an Icelandic postcard thanking Megan for the flies saying that her flies took the Icelandic salmon completely by storm. "3 of us had 53 fish in 3½ days, 30 on Arndilly Fancy and six on Lady Seafield."

A fish of 35lb was taken from the Upper Pot on the Lower Brora on 30 May 1957 by an angler fishing with one of Megan's flies, a No. 8 Black Doctor. The photo records it being hooked at 9.15pm and grassed at 10.15; unfortunately there is no record of the captor.

Some of Megan's "friends" just like to pass the time of day in their thankyou letters and one such angler wrote from his home on Aberdeen Deeside saying that the

*autumn colours here on the Dee are spectacular just now – and quite a few fish up for spawning – at last a lovely spell of quiet warm dry weather and river back to normal.*

It is a mark of the close-knit community in which Megan lived that the postman never failed her. One of her early customers addressed his letter, dated 27 April 1949, to:

*The Lady who Ties Salmon Flies (I think Miss Megan), Brora, Sutherland.*

Needless to say the letter arrived safely. The writer remarked:

*I saw your card at Oykel Bridge when fishing there last year and George Ross (Head Ghillie on the Oykel) spoke highly of your flies.*

The writer then went on to order 20 flies including Black Doctor, Mar Lodge, Wilkinson, Thunder and Lightning, Yellow Torrish, Jock Scott, Blue Charm and Dusty Miller.

With the exception of the Blue Charm, I [DM] doubt whether any of the other patterns would be used much nowadays.

She received so many letters from the U.S.A. thanking her for her flies and remarking on how beautifully they were tied that it is difficult to single out any particular letter. But there is one that has a unique charm:

*Dear Miss Boyd, It had been a long day, one of many over a period of months, and frankly I was tired and somewhat depressed over the loss of a large computer sale to a competitor. Your lovely letter, the clippings and the most beautiful salmon fly I've ever seen changed my mood to one of joy.*

# Chapter Seven

# An Honour
# is Bestowed

In January 1971 Megan was awarded the British Empire Medal (BEM) in the Queen's New Year Honour List. She wrote to Her Majesty explaining that she would be unable to attend the Investiture at Buckingham Palace, as she had no one to look after her dog. The presentation was therefore held at the Burghfield Hotel, Dornoch where Lord Migdale, Lord Lieutenant of Sutherland, presented her with her medal.

Lord Migdale was accompanied by his daughter, Miss Margaret Thomson. Others present included Mr Donald McBain, County Convenor, and Mrs McBain, Mrs Helen MacLennan, wife of the constituency M.P. and Major Alec Neish, clerk to the Lord Lieutenant, and Mrs Neish.

Before the presentation Miss Boyd handed Lord Migdale a selection of salmon flies which she had made herself and which she had specially named Clydesdale and Fluffy Feet (a reference to Miss Thomson's thoroughbred horses at her farm at Ospisdale), Migdale, Brora, Helmsdale, Sunrise and Sutherland. The dressings for some of these are given in the chapter on Fly Dressings (*see* pages 38-39).

Lord Migdale read a letter from the Queen regretting that she was unable to present the award personally.

Megan had the honour of many visits from Prince Charles when he came north to fish the Helmsdale River. On one occasion one of his friends wrote to Megan prior to the Prince's visit:

*The Prince of Wales has asked me to write to you to see if it is possible for you to tie him some flies such as you recently tied for me. He greatly admired them when he saw them and thought that they were exactly what he needed for Spring fishing.*

*If you do not recall my order, it was basically for the normal patterns as used in the Helmsdale, the yellow and black flies, the orange flies with the golden shank, Thunder and Lightning and possibly one other typical Helmsdale pattern.*

*I would rather that you did not mention about the Prince of Wales to anyone at all as there is a danger that the news might leak out and he might be pestered by Press during his visit to the Helmsdale this year. We did have slight problems with the Press last year.*

Megan received visits at her cottage from Prince Charles and on one occasion they had a discussion about the fly called the Popham which was considered to be very good. She also received invitations to visit him while he was up fishing the Helmsdale.

On one occasion Megan tied a fly to mark Prince Charles' birthday and the dressing is as follows:

| | |
|---|---|
| **Hook** | Size 12/0 |
| **Tag** | Silver & red, white & blue floss |
| **Tail** | Golden pheasant & red, white & blue swan |
| **Body** | Blue, red & yellow seals fur |
| **Ribs** | Flat silver & gold twist each side of flat silver |
| **Throat** | Yellow golden eagle |
| **Wings** | 2 jungle cock, 2 tippets either side, strips of argus topping |
| **Sides** | Jungle cock |
| **Cheeks** | Kingfisher |
| **Horns** | Blue & red macaw |
| **Head** | Black |

# CHAPTER EIGHT

# Those Who Knew Her

## Gloria Younger

The first time I met Megan was in the early Sixties at a Scottish Country Dance Rally. I didn't know then that I was making friends with the finest maker of classic salmon flies in the world.

Over the following years we continued to meet at various country dances, and it was only then that I discovered that she tied salmon flies for a living and was famous throughout the world.

By a strange coincidence my husband James (Jimmy to everyone else) was also a flydresser and had

Megan Boyd's featherwing flies were remarkable for their balance, colour and overall neatness. Feathers were paired carefully to give a precise symmetry to each fly. The flies in this photo were tied for presentation, but all flies sold under Megan's name reflected this level of perfection.

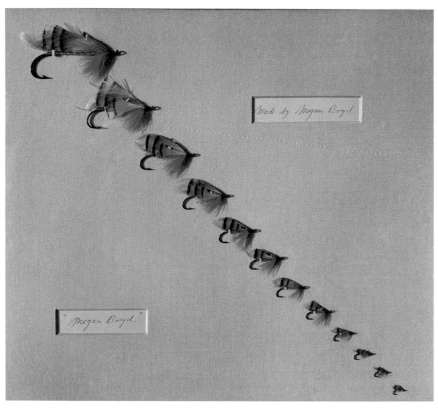

An impressive display of 'Megan Boyd' flies, tied by Megan herself in a range of sizes. This collection is owned by the writer David Profumo who, as a boy, sat at Megan's tying table.

The 'Megan Boyd', a fly suggested to Megan by her friends Gloria and Jimmy Younger and which reflected Megan's favourite colours.

Megan with her dog, Punch, on the hill behind her house at Kintradwell overlooking the North Sea.

Many of Megan's regular customers would turn up at her door, often unannounced, and would place their orders for more flies, or collect a previously ordered batch before going fishing on one of the many great salmon rivers near to Brora.

Putting the finishing twists of thread to one of her famous featherwing salmon flies.

A fine brace of springers taken from the Brora, the river closest to where Megan lived.

Megan's isolated house at Kintradwell, near Brora, in 2012.

Megan Boyd tyings from a collection belonging to David Profumo

Covent Garden     Lord Migdale     Sutherland

Blue Doctor     Megan Boyd     Member

Jock Scott     Helmsdale Doctor     Orange Parson

Dunkeld     Scalscraggie     Thistle

A selection of flies tied by Megan for an edition of Thomas Edwin Pryce-Tannatt's *How to Dress Salmon Flies*.

Childers

Dreadnought

Blue Limerick

Black Prince

Colonel Bates

Sutherland

Megan's distinctive kidney-shaped flytying desk on which, over the course of her long career, she tied thousands of salmon flies. The desk was sold at auction soon after Megan died.

The artist at work, surrounded by feather capes, furs, hooks, threads and tinsels – and pictures of canine friends.

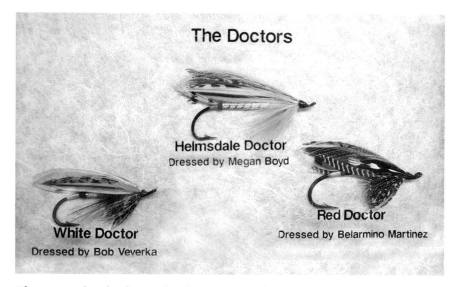

**The Doctors**

Helmsdale Doctor
Dressed by Megan Boyd

Red Doctor
Dressed by Belarmino Martinez

White Doctor
Dressed by Bob Veverka

Photograph of a framed selection of salmon flies all with the word 'Doctor' incorporated into their names. Megan's dressing of the predominantly yellow Helmsdale Doctor was a very popular choice among the Helmsdale regulars. *(courtesy of American Museum of Fly Fishing, Vermont)*

Below: A selection of salmon flies tied by Megan for her good friend Orri Vigfusson.

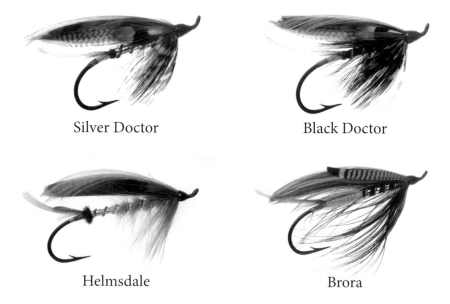

Silver Doctor

Black Doctor

Helmsdale

Brora

served his apprenticeship with well-known firms in Kelso and Glasgow.

In 1967 James was offered a job as manager of the "Sutherland Fly Company" in Helmsdale and, after we married in 1968, we moved to Brora to live. We passed Megan's home every day as we travelled to and from work in Helmsdale where I was a hairdresser as she lived about two miles outside Brora on the Helmsdale road. We would call in to see her quite often to see how she was and catch up with local gossip!

She loved cars and owned over the years many different models, the first being an Austin in 1938. During the war she was a part-time warden and was allocated a motorcycle combination (that is the motorcycle with a side-car) to carry out her duties.

Megan supported many charities and often arranged or took part in fund-raising events in the region. In 1971 she was awarded the B.E.M. (British Empire Medal).

In 1969 James was offered a job as manager of a large flydressing company in Hong Kong. We returned to the U.K. in 1976 and went to live at Durness in Sutherland. Megan would visit us on a Sunday along with one or two of her friends. "Just out for a run" she would say, although it was a journey of well over a 100 miles!

When we moved to Dumfries in 1979 we didn't see her as often but still kept in touch by post.

If you visited Megan during the day or early evening, and she was busy at work with a special order, you would be sent to the kitchen to make the tea for yourself (and for herself of course!)

Much has been written about Megan's workbench over the years. When James cleared out her workshop in 1989 after she had died, he managed to salvage it and it was in our kitchen for many years supporting a hi-fi music system! As it has woodworm we contemplated burning it but we just couldn't do it. However, one day we saw in the papers that an agent from Bonham's would be in the area. We contact the firm and it was duly collected and put up for auction. I was happy that it found a new home.

Along with the workbench, James saved hundreds of letters from all over the world, also order books, invoices and receipt books, some dating back to 1947. In fact Megan's life can be followed from the paperwork she left.

Although Megan lived on her own she was never lonely and she had many visitors who would come for a chat and, of course, during the fishing season, there would always be her customers either collecting their flies or leaving new orders.

Megan was a very kind person and would go out of her way to help others. I was privileged to know Megan and be her friend for over 40 years. Some of my happiest memories were when we visited Megan when she wasn't working but sitting in the large bay window of her house, just enjoying the peace and quiet, the stunning view and putting the world to rights.

After reading the letters to Megan I can appreciate how much she meant to so many people and the joy she brought to them with her wonderful flies.

# David Profumo

Back in 1970, I was a pustulated youth with lank locks and a head full of Deep Purple, but the one thing that escaped my generalised hatred of the world was fishing. My uncle had a sporting estate in Sutherland, and one day my mother paid a call, unannounced, on Megan Boyd at her coastal home nearby at Kintradwell, and they struck up a friendship. Megan recognised my mother (who, before marriage ended her career, had been the actress Valerie Hobson) and they shared a love for ballet and dancing; before long Megan heard of the unruly adolescent with his sole passion for fishing, and an invitation was procured for me to go and visit her.

I was led, somewhat apprehensively, into her tying room - no electricity, the kidney-shaped dressing table where she worked, the aroma of mothballs and wax – and this curious-looking lady with her severe haircut, shirt and tie, but inexpressibly delicate fingers and gentle demeanour, began to introduce me properly to the intricacies of a craft which, in her hands, had surely been elevated to an art form.

At her request, I had brought along a couple of boxes of my own flies - battle-scarred Wheatleys passed on to me by the venerable Uncle - and she was a stern critic of my ghastly, self-taught efforts. In truth, I had very little notion of the business of constructing flies, having begun with a simple Veniards starter kit. I was less than dexterous, knew little of piscatorial history, but I became entranced.

Over the course of repeated visits, two summers in a row, I beheld her handiwork, and was encouraged to attempt to follow her methods. Megan was a stickler for the correct materials in tying the classic patterns – Pryce-Tannatt's *How to Dress Salmon Flies* (1914) was her professional Bible, and she made sure I secured a copy of my own – and she used the complex, original dressing of the Jock Scott as her gold standard (I still treasure the first one she tied for me as a demonstration) and she gave me some precious, rare feathers such as summer duck, Florican bustard and toucan, along with a bag of olden times long-shank hooks that went up to a size 12/0 (a low-water iron!).

My own efforts were concentrated more on simpler patterns such as the Hairy Mary, and I spent frustrating hours working on keeping the body bulk down, and getting my heads neater. It must have been pretty boring for her, but she had immaculate manners and was always politeness personified – another fine example she set.

Megan was effectively at the end of a line of traditional artisans, but she never tied purely virtuoso dressings (I wonder what she would have made of the outlandish 'catwalk creations' that exhibition dressers produce these days, some without even conventional hooks), and she rarely made things for collectors or mere display, though her side table was festooned with correspondence from across the globe, placing orders and, doubtless, seeking favours. Her flies were primarily for fishing with – though, famously, she had never cast a line herself. She was considerably amused by the earnest antics of anglers, who brought all manner of ingenious ideas to her shack to be incorporated into fancy dressings – eyebrows, bits of pet parrot, and on one occasion a ball of silver paper (a Brora rod had tossed his scrumpled Kit Kat wrapper into the stream and a fish had promptly snaffled it). "There's no-one more silly than a fisherman," she liked to remark, though she never said anything like that to her ungainly teenaged apprentice.

She never charged anything for her lessons, either, but my mother used to bring her little presents by way of a thank-you. I realised even then, despite the obscuring fug of adolescent hormones, that I was in the presence of someone truly exceptional, and that it was a privilege. I certainly tried my level best, but I doubt she was ever exactly proud of her latest pupil's hungover-looking hairwings.

My mother continued to correspond with Megan long after my Uncle's estate was sold, and I had flown the nest. She persuaded her to tie two series of flies for me, which Megan knew were destined for framing (she signed them and seemed happy that they would be going to a good home.)

First, a selection of fully dressed, built-wing Scottish flies such as the Torrish, Lord Migdale and Durham Ranger (one of her favourites) on 2/0 hooks; also she produced an array of flies from a 10/0 down to a size 12 all in a pattern of her own devising called the Megan Boyd. This was nothing to do with that frumpier, but piscicidal, dark wispy pattern that is sometimes sold with her name attached and is popular in Iceland – this Megan dressing is a resplendent, tinselly concoction of orange and lime green, which she told me was modelled on the costume of a Covent Garden ballet dancer she had seen (presumably in an illustration). I have never come across this particular pattern anywhere else, and I very much doubt it would have been of much commercial appeal. I have these two sets framed and named, in my Perthshire tackle room, as an enduring inspiration to my erstwhile mentor.

As is well known, the years of working without artificial light took their toll on Megan, and her eyesight began to fail around 1985. My mother persuaded her to tie a selection of number 12 singles to frame as a Christening present for our first son, who was born that year. I believe these must therefore be amongst the very last tiny salmon flies she ever produced (she lost her eyesight in 1988, I think). I regret I never saw Megan again, in her old age, but the patterns she made me at the height of her powers are like the Fabergés of the flydresser's art.

I am told individual examples of her work fetch hundreds of pounds at auction; mine are entirely worthless, being but a journeyman's tools for the job. I will never forget her kindliness and patience. Except as a hackle shade, I'm not sure she had ever heard of Deep Purple.

The author **David Profumo** is Fishing Correspondent on *Country Life* magazine

# Orri Vigfusson

Scotland's Megan Boyd, who died on 15 November 2001, was hailed by many as the finest tyer of fishing flies in the world. Despite the huge numbers of salmon that could not resist her flies, she never fished herself.

Miss Boyd, of Brora in Sutherland, began tying flies at the age of 12 under the expert tutelage of a Sutherland keeper, Bob Trussler, and quickly became an artist in the craft. She made her reputation by tying classic and traditional flies like the Jock Scott, Silver Doctor, Durham Ranger and Wilkinson. She rarely bothered to invent a new tying though some of the most complicated patterns that she tied can only be produced by an expert of her calibre.

Megan, however, did give the angling world one creation that will ensure that salmon fishermen never forget her name. With the help of a friend and a client, Jim Pilkington, she devised a fly that became widely known as the Megan Boyd and it became her trademark in dealing with fishermen around the world.

This small fly catches fish whether tied in the normal manner on a single hook or as a tube fly. Many fishermen swear that a tiny Megan Boyd, which she dressed on a minute tube with a size 18 treble, will catch salmon in dead low summer flows when most anglers would not expect any sport. Carefully used, with a gentle touch, these little flies have often saved some of Megan Boyd's more knowledgeable customers from a blank day!

For over half a century she worked in her garden shed at Kintradwell, overlooking the North Sea. A kidney-shaped dressing table served as her workbench and on it she tied flies with the meticulous precision that was described in a letter printed by the *Inverness Courier*. Jimmie Ferard, who has collected her work for many years and still has over 2,000 of her flies, wrote: 'Her flytying was unique. Surely one of the world's greatest perfectionists in this art.'

He added: *'The trouble she took over just arranging the pieces of hair for a Stoat's Tail fly had to be seen to be believed. She used to put these hairs in the top of her lipstick holder with the ends sticking out and she said they should never be trimmed or cut as this was unnatural to the fish.'*

In 1971 Megan received the British Empire Medal, the highest honour ever awarded to any flytyer. For most of her life she was full of energy and she was a much-loved local figure. Country dancing was her favourite relaxation though she also enjoyed playing bridge. She took an active role in helping the old and disabled locally, giving them lifts when required and she worked constantly to enhance the life of her village.

I first met her in her shed in 1985 when at last the local electric company had brought electricity to her house. No wonder her eyesight was failing! Then she drove me into the village for some special biscuits she wanted to give my children. Though she had already turned 70 she just threw on the safety belt and drove like mad. A few years later she was forced to give up her work and had to retire from the vice at which she had tied so many wonderful flies.

Each time I travelled to the northern part of Scotland I made a point of visiting her. We shared many interests in rural life and country pursuits. We would sit and reminisce and recount many things associated with the lifestyles of small communities in Scotland and Iceland.

But always the talk came back to salmon flies and their history, the dressings and the vast number of renowned fishermen friends she had made during her lifetime. Yes, she remembered Charles H. Akroyd, the veteran sportsman from Duncraggie, Brora, who devised the Akroyd fly, sometimes called the poor man's Jock Scott. He visited Iceland's Laxá in Aôaldalur (Big Laxá) river way back in 1877.

Megan, a true expert, loved to talk about the art of flytying. Her flies had to be exactly right. The shape, the material, the lengths and sizes all mattered terribly.

Nobody really knows why the salmon takes a fly. I remember discussing this with her at length and we always came back to the baby sand eels on which young salmon smolts feed when they first leave their natal rivers at the start of their oceanic migration.

She and I were both worried because Scotland's sand eel shoals were suffering badly from the industrial trawlers that were scooping the little fish up from the east coast sandbanks literally outside her window.

Many anglers believe that the reactions of a salmon that takes their fly are triggered by infant memories of its first encounters with the abundant food source that sand eels can provide.

The precision and deftness of the flytyer may be more important in the mind of the angler than to the fish though there is no doubt that the colour of the fly, its sinuosity in water and its size play a much greater role in its success. The actual presentation of the fly is also vital. Salmon, like birds, want to protect their habitat in the river and will fight foreign objects that trespass on their space.

Last year the Prince of Wales honoured Megan with a visit and she told me that they had discussed the Popham, a very great fly. She said that if she had to pick a favourite, this glorious creation would be her choice. Originated by F.L. Popham, this pattern is one of the most complicated and beautifully constructed of all the classic dressings that Britain has given to the sport.

'A challenge at the vise and a fine addition to any collection, with its veiling of tiny Indian crow feathers' according to Col. Joseph D. Bates and his daughter Pamela Bates Richards.

I met Megan this summer for the last time in the comfortable old folk's home in Golspie to which she had retired. She received every care at the home and the dedicated helpers there put my flowers in a vase as she greeted me. As ever she was smartly dressed and wearing the tie she often adopted. Without her tying vice and her flies I think she had become tired of life but even if she did feel there was little left to live for she never really complained. We talked for hours as she relived the past. She put up a brave face and would not let go of my hand. 'Life has been good to me,' she declared.

Megan Boyd was the youngest of three children. She was born in England, in 1915 it is thought but was taken to Scotland in 1918 when her father became a bailiff or river watcher on a Sutherland estate. She never married. During World War II Megan had a variety of jobs that included a spell as a milk-roundswoman and duties as an Auxiliary Coastguard. Though she probably did not have much formal education she was never at a loss in dealing with her many distinguished customers.

As a dedicated conservationist Megan was a major supporter of the North Atlantic Salmon Fund (NASF) and its efforts to buy out all the salmon nets that prevent the small stocks of wild salmon that remain from reaching their native rivers to spawn. She regularly donated wonderful examples of her flies to be auctioned around the world to help the NASF cause.

Megan Boyd, the consummate practitioner of her craft, will always be remembered by flytyers all over the world. I am sure that if it were possible, they would erect a proud memorial to her artistry at the main gate of the anglers' Valhalla.

**Orri Vigfusson** is Chairman of the North Atlantic Salmon Fund.

# Glyn Satterley

I first met Megan Boyd at a whist drive in Brora, Sutherland. I was doing a project on 'Life in Caithness and Sutherland', which was eventually made into my first book. I am no card sharp, but was there specifically to meet Megan, and hopefully get permission to photograph her at work. I was looking for well-known local characters, and Megan, I was told, was a 'must'. Megan being Megan greeted me with warmth, and didn't hesitate. "Come and see me tomorrow."

I arrived at her house and workshop just up from the beach, the following morning. She was immensely generous with her time, and I think a tad flattered at being photographed. She was also very helpful – moving her head, hands, flies or materials whenever and wherever I asked. As a very inexperienced snapper, I was not as decisive as I could have been, but she was very patient with me.

Her 'workshop' was nothing more than a modest garden shed situated at the side of the house, but inside it was a visual Aladdin's Cave. At the far end where Megan worked, the bench-top was covered with thread, wool, yarn, silk, tinsel, nylon, wire, varnish, glue, hair, fur, deer skin, wax, scissors, tweezers, hooks of all sizes and a multitude of flies – some on racks, some scattered in front of her. Feathers of all kinds coloured the surface, including Indian crow, toucan, turkey, mallard, bustard, peacock, swan, blue chatterer, blue macaw, golden pheasant and many more. I even spotted a whole mallard wing. At the door end of the shed, her worktop was submerged under a mountain of opened envelopes, each containing orders for flies and in many cases payment as well. Pinned on the wall above her worktop was a gallery of doggy calendars and prints. She was a real dog lover.

Megan sat on a stool at her work-bench with Patch her small scruffy terrier, curled up beneath her feet. The little Calor Gas heater behind her, aimed at her feet, was the only source of heating. Right in front of her bench the shed windows facing south were her main source of light. I learnt she only worked while daylight was good enough – up to fourteen hours in summer, in winter far fewer. The view from her windows was inspirational to her. She never tired of gazing out onto the strand of sand and the breaking waves. She often told me "Nowhere in the world can compare to this."

While working at her bench Megan looked so self-assured, calm and resolute. As an Art student I had studied films of artists at work and watching Megan in those days reminded me both of Picasso, with his total belief and self-confidence, and Fabergé, for his precision and tireless striving to create the most beautiful, elegant objects. I have since photographed many artists and craftsmen, and it is rare to find the genuine article, true masters of their trade, as Megan so obviously was.

She just sat there weaving her magic; everything she needed thoughtfully placed within arm's length. She selected and tied small pieces of feather, wound thread, moulded tiny strips of foil, tied knots meticulously, snipped twine, dabbed varnish – it was mesmerising. I did far more watching than photographing. Her skills were honed from having tied literally thousands of flies since the age of twelve, and working years of long summer days. She was sixty-three when I first met her, but she was hard to age. She used to say:

*"Attention to detail is critical."*
*"You have to make a good job"*
*"Above all else I like to be accurate."*

Her work ethic was flawless.

Megan's hands were surprisingly large, not at all delicate for someone who worked with such precision.

*"I haven't got fine hands, but it's like everything else, if you really want to do a thing your hands don't matter."*

Easy for her to say!

Above all else, she cared passionately that her flies looked and worked as they should. There was however an irreconcilable conflict within her, because Megan hated the idea that her flies led ultimately to the death of a salmon.

At times she was somewhat disparaging of fishermen:

*"I'm not bothered about the fish, or the fishermen. I just love tying a fly, and I like to make a good job because it looks attractive to me."*

Or

*"There's nothing so stupid as a fisherman. Do you think a fish cares whether a fly is well tied or not?"*

On occasions she would go along with 'their delusions' just to keep them quiet. One Helmsdale fisherman had crumpled the silver foil from inside his cigarette packet, and thrown it into the river causing a fish to rise. Megan was quickly asked to make a 'similar' style fly, which she did, with her tongue in her cheek, and the angler went away happy.

Megan's house was a dark red and white corrugated iron bungalow, just north of Brora, built in 1906 and owned by the Kintradwell estate. It had no electricity, no running water, only bottled gas for lighting and no phone. Water was either carried by bucket from the burn, or brought back from Brora. Cups of tea often entailed a visit to the burn first.

From the outside it looked pretty smart, and inside with its flowery wallpaper décor it appeared cosy, and just about windproof and weather-tight. The main reason for this was that Megan was a dab hand at D.I.Y, adept at doing her own joinery and decorating. She was proud to show off her handiwork, which included several chairs and lamps she had made. She was also good at literally papering over cracks that appeared on the inside walls. Whatever, I know she loved it there, and enjoyed her independent lifestyle.

After that first visit, we became friends, and I returned many times over the next seven years, not always to take photographs, but often simply dropping in for a chat and a cup of tea. I would often pass her house while heading north to photograph in the Helmsdale Strath or en route to Caithness. She always made me welcome and enjoyed our chats, and as she had no phone I used to pitch up unannounced. If the Renault 4 was by the house, I knew she was in. If she was out I wrote a message in the notebook she left by her front door. This was primarily for fishermen to leave their orders for flies.

Occasionally she would ask where I was heading, and if I could drop off a package of flies, to various lodges or hotels on my journey northwards. It was a pleasure to help her, and small thanks for all the hospitality she had shown me.

On a couple of summer visits I met her sister April, who came up from the south annually to stay with Megan. She was a lovely lady, totally in awe of her distinguished sister, and intrigued by her lifestyle, particularly the water collection from the burn. Megan was very fond of her.

A special and memorable visit for me was when I introduced Megan to my new wife, Andrea, in the autumn of 1982. She made us tremendously welcome, with a feast of cheese, biscuits and cake specially prepared and served in the front room of the house.

We could sense her excitement and delight.

Sundays were 'no go' because Megan was out. She never worked on a Sunday, and spent most of them touring around Sutherland in her old Renault, generously giving friends, or local old or disabled folks a day out.

She was extremely kind and caring. However, she cared for animals and people in equal measure, and was regularly in conflict with members of the local crofting club, who reared sheep on the ground around her house. She was often appalled at their 'rough' treatment of stock, and let them know it. She occasionally took under her wing injured or sickly lambs, and nursed them till they recovered.

Megan's 'eccentric' but smart appearance, wearing shirt and tie, tweed jacket and skirt, v-necked sweater, heavy leather shoes, and self-cut bobbed hair often disarmed people who did not know her. It threw me slightly when I met her, but after my first visit I never gave it another thought. She was a lovely, genuine, caring and giving person, who was uniquely gifted, and that was all that mattered. She was a gem.

Away from the house and workshop and off-duty, one saw another side to Megan. She was full of life and energy and very sociable. As far as I know she didn't drink, but she didn't need to, she knew how to party without it!

She loved country dancing with a passion and went at least once a week throughout the winter months. On a couple of occasions she let me accompany her with the main intention of getting some pictures. Photography ended up taking a back seat, while I was bowled around with gusto for much of the evening, by Megan and her friends. It was exhausting, but much fun and laughter was had. Sadly few images exist.

I did accompany her to another whist drive once. She was a mean card player and reputedly a good bridge player too. Again she made sure I joined in the action, and I spent the evening being passed from table to table, much to her amusement. Megan revelled in these local group activities and was a popular participant.

The last time I popped in to see Megan at her cottage, she had been diagnosed with macular degeneration and her sight was failing. She had just returned from London, where a group of her River Helmsdale patrons had paid for her to go and visit an eye specialist. Sadly she had been told her vision would continue to deteriorate as it had been doing for the last few years. She had by then stopped tying flies.

I saw her on one other occasion at the nursing home in Brora, where she moved to before her death in 2001. In spite of seriously diminishing sight, Megan greeted me with a broad and cheery smile, and a hand-shake that was still as strong as ever. God bless her.

**Glyn Satterley** is a professional photographer who works throughout the Highlands. He has has several books to his name including *Life in Caithness & Sutherland*, *The Highland Game* and, most recently, *Going to the Hill*.

# CHAPTER NINE

# The End of a Legend

*And then, to lose your sight because you looked too hard,*
*for too long, in rooms without electricity,*
*without adequate illumination,*
*to be undone by what has shaped you.*
– Kiss the Water

Megan's eyesight must have been troubling her for some time before she retired and evidence for this is seen in a letter from one of her visitors, who was a consultant orthopaedic surgeon, in October 1984:

*You may remember that my friend and I visited you last August when on holiday in Brora. I have very happy recollections of the morning we spent listening to you and watching you at work.*

> *My parting question was to ask if you needed anything, which was unobtainable locally, and you said you needed magnifying spectacles for your tying. I have now managed to obtain a pair of spectacles similar to those I sometimes use myself for tying smaller trout flies and I hope you will accept them from one of your admirers.*

In a letter to one of her customers there was also evidence that her flytying days were reaching an end:

> *I am very sorry I cannot tie the set of Scrope's flies for you. Some years ago I tied a set for ASJ (Atlantic Salmon Journal) library stating then that would be the last set I would tie. Perhaps you can photograph the enclosed then please return.*
>
> *I have had over 50 years tying and I would like to see someone else with a genuine desire to tie a good classic fly taking over.*
>
> *My waiting list is now 3 years with orders ranging from 12 – 180. One day I hope to give all these people 2 flies each – the demand for this sort of work has become a worry to me and I feel very sad having to refuse a request from anyone.*

Jimmy and Gloria Younger had made frequent visits to Megan since they'd left Brora and knew that she was no longer tying flies and not keeping fit. However, the following letter, dated 24th June 1988, says everything:

*Dear Jimmy and Gloria,*
*Just a scrawl to the best of my ability as I am sad to tell you I can no longer tie a fly or see one properly. I lost my dear dog the beginning of the year and then my eyes just went. Hardening of the arteries behind the eyes – no cure, no glasses and not good.*

*I have just got a sheltered house in the village just one bedroom and hope to be in end July or beginning of August. April is here and done all the packing for me... My workshop and contents are just left, as I hate setting foot in there again. Have given Jim's name to my customers. I made out my Will a while ago and left all my stuff to Jimmy except the Kelson book I promised to Colin Simpson as I did promise it to him long ago now and I hate going back on a promise. [sadly, the book was taken by some unscrupulous overseas folk who came to visit Megan when she was in the home and almost blind]*

*Well that is all my problems now I hope you are both well. Come and see me when you are up north.*
*My best regards and good wishes to you both.*
*Love from Megan*

*PS. April sends her love.*

A telegram from Prince Charles dated 24th May (1988) found with her papers, says:

> *"I was very sad to learn that failing eyesight has forced you to abandon the craft at which you so excelled. I know that your skill will be missed amongst the fly fishing community but your many friends will now be glad to see your return to Brora. I did want to send you every good wish."*

In a poignant draft note to Prince Charles, Megan offers good wishes to him and Lady Diana for their marriage and wishes them "a lifetime of peace and happiness." The note accompanied a fly, which she asks Prince Charles to give to Lady Diana. She adds:

> *"Tell her you now have the best catch you will ever have…"*

Megan lived on for some years and was always busy in the community to the best of her ability. Although blind she could still recognise one of the flies that she had tied by simply feeling the head of the fly.

She died in hospital in Golspie on 15 November 2001 at the age of 86. As Larry Borders said while she was alive: "She is among a dying breed of 'original' artists to whom the tying of beautiful flies is still a labour of love."

Watching the film on Megan's life (*Kiss the Water*) where Jimmy made a fleeting appearance, we were saddened to see the state of her house and workshop.

She will be remembered by all her friends from around the world – from Australia, Japan, practically all the states in the USA, Canada, Iceland, Norway, Sweden, Holland, Belgium, France, Spain, Germany and of course throughout the United Kingdom.

When the late Joseph Bates, author of a number of books on Atlantic salmon flies, asked many well-known salmon anglers who were the best salmon flydressers he replied that the best were in Scotland and Megan Boyd was the best of them all.

Her funeral service was held in Clyne Free Church and the Reverend Ken Hunter made splendid reference to her gifts in her chosen craft and to her social qualities. Her friend, Brora rod-maker and tackle dealer Rob Wilson, called it a fitting farewell to a great Highland character, from England.

Since 1928, when Megan tied her first fly, the art of flytying has become an increasingly popular pastime as well as a lucrative business. There are now Fly Fairs at which exponents of the art exchange ideas and sell flytying materials and demonstrate the intricacies of the art to a growing number of enthusiasts keen to learn. A significant proportion are young anglers anxious to tie their own flies and go down to the water to catch a fish on "one of their own making."

Megan would smile.

The End

# Acknowledgements

This account of Megan Boyd's life as a salmon flydresser could never have been written had she not left all her correspondence relating to flydressing to Jimmy Younger.

We are most grateful to a number of people who so generously spent so much time to provide fascinating accounts of their meetings with Megan Boyd. David Profumo tells of his time as a youth being shown the intricacies of dressing classic featherwing salmon flies; Orri Vigfusson, in recording his friendship with Megan, demonstrates his fondness of her and his courtesy towards her on his visits from Iceland. Glyn Satterley, a professional photographer, describes in depth his many experiences with Megan – tying flies, playing bridge, even country dancing. Gloria Younger had a long friendship with Megan and shared her love of animals and dancing. We thank them all.

Peter Veniard very kindly allowed us to print the *Importation of Plumage (Prohibition) Act 1921* notice and also a copy of an invoice for flytying material sent by his firm to Megan Boyd.

We are most indebted to Orri Vigfusson for contributing photos of his collection of flies dressed by

Megan Boyd, Larus Karl Ingason took the photos of these flies and Kristin Robertsdottir transmitted the images. We are also most grateful to David Profumo for the photos of some of his flies tied by Megan, and to Glyn Satterley for photographing them.

We wish to thank Sara Wilcox, Director of Visual Communications and Yoki Akayama, Deputy Director, both of the American Museum of Fly Fishing, (Manchester, Vermont, USA) for providing photos of the displays of some of Megan Boyd's flies in their collection.

We appreciate Gareth Evans' kindness for giving us permission to use his words composed for the pamphlet that accompanies the DVD of the film *Kiss the Water*, produced by BBC Scotland.

Derek Mills & Jimmy Younger

# Also published by Merlin Unwin Books

**Nymphing – the new way** Jonathan White £20

**The Healing Stream** Laurence Catlow £20

**GT – a flyfisher's guide to Giant Trevally**
Peter McLeod £30

**Flycasting Skills** John Symonds £9.99

**How to Fish** John Symonds £9.99

**Trout from a Boat** Dennis Moss £16

**Pocket Guide to Matching the Hatch**
Peter Lapsley and Cyril Bennett £7.99

**Pocket Guide to Fishing Knots**
Step-by-Step Coarse, Sea and Game Knots
Peter Owen £5.99

**Beginner's Guide to Flytying**
Chris Mann and Terry Griffiths £9.99

**Complete Illustrated Directory of Salmon Flies**
Chris Mann £20

**Trout in Dirty Places** Theo Pike £20

**Once a Flyfisher** Laurence Catlow £17.99

**The Fisherman's Bedside Book** BB £18.95

**Canal Fishing** Dominic Garnett £20

**Flyfishing for Coarse Fish** Dominic Garnett £20

**Fishing with Harry** Tony Baws £15.99

**Fishing with Emma** David Overland £9.99

**Flies of Ireland** Peter O'Reilly £20

full details: www.merlinunwin.co.uk